THE GREATEST
JEWISH
TENNIS
PLAYERS
OF ALL TIME

THE GREATEST JEWISH TENNIS PLAYERS OF ALL TIME

SANDRA HARWITT
New Chapter Press

The Greatest Jewish Tennis Players of All Time is published by New Chapter Press (www.NewChapterMedia.com) and distributed by the IPG (www.IPGBook.com)

For more information on this title or New Chapter Press contact:

Randy Walker
Managing Partner
New Chapter Press

1175 York Ave
Suite #3s
New York, NY 10065
Rwalker@NewChapterMedia.com

ISBN: 978-1937559366

Photo of Baron Umberto Louis de Morpurgo courtesy of Robert Fuller and the Silver Tennis Collection; Photo of Daniel Prenn courtesy of the German Federal Archives; Photo of Ladislav Hecht courtesy of WikiCommons; Photo of Suzy Kormoczy courtesy of the Jewish Sports Hall of Fame; Photo of Dick Savitt courtesy of Getty Images; Photo of Herb Flam courtesy of UCLA; Photo of Pierre Darmon courtesy of the ITF; Photo of Angela Buxton courtesy of the Jewish Sports Hall of Fame; Photo of Renee Richards courtesy of WikiCommons; Photo of Allen Fox courtesy of Allen Fox; Photo of Tom Okker courtesy of WikiCommons; Photo of Julie Heldman courtesy of Stanford University; Photo of Brian Gottfried courtesy of Fred Mullane of CameraWorkUSA, Photo of Harold Solomon courtesy of Fred Mullane of CameraWorkUSA; Photo of Brian Teacher courtesy of TennisAustralia; Photo of Michael Fishbach courtesy of Fred Mullane of CameraWorkUSA; Photo of Ilana Kloss courtesy of Mylan WorldTeamTennis; Photo of Shlomo Glickstein courtesy of the Israeli Government Press Office; Photo of Eliot Teltscher courtesy of Fred Mullane of CameraWorkUSA; Photo of Van Winitsky courtesy of the ATP; Photo of Brad Gilbert courtesy of Robbie Mendelson on WikiCommons; Photo of Elise Burgin is courtesy of Stanford University; Photo of Jim Grabb courtesy of Stanford University; Photo of Martin Jaite courtesy of Fred Mullane of CameraWorkUSA; Photo of Amos Mansdorf courtesy of the Israeli Government Press Office; Photo of Jay Berger courtesy of the USTA; Photo of Aaron Krickstein courtesy of Fred Mullane of CameraWorkUSA; Photo of Anna Smashanova courtesy of Jameboy on WikiCommons; Photo of Justin Gimelstob courtesy of UCLA; Photo of Jonathan Erlich and Andy Ram courtesy of Phil98 of WikiCommons; Photo of Nicolas Massu courtesy of Cecilia Pérez Jara on WikiCommons; Photo of Scott Lipsky courtesy of Stanford University; Photo of Noam Gershony courtesy of robbiesaurus on WikiCommons; Photo of Shahar Peer courtesy of Keith Allison of WikiCommons; Photo of Jesse Levine courtesy of Bridget Samuels of CreativeCommons; Photo of Julie Glushko courtesy of Stefan Brending via CreativeCommons (http://creativecommons.org/licenses/by-sa/3.0/d...). New Chapter Press would also like to thank Brian Risso of Stanford University, Danny Harrington of UCLA, Tim Curry with the USTA, Rosie Crews of Mylan World Team Tennis, Joe Siegman of the International Jewish Sports Hall of Fame, Patricia Jensen, Ben Sturner and, most sincerely Fred and Susan Mullane for their assistance.

*To Four People Who Have Made My
Life Special & Filled With Love*

My parents, Ernest & Gloria Harwitt

&

*My nephew, Michael H Weber, and
niece, Alicia Weber Neveloff*

TABLE OF CONTENTS

FOREWORD
By Harold Solomon

I was really fortunate to come to tennis in its infancy as a professional sport. I followed in the path of many incredibly great players and like to think I helped open the door even wider for those stars who followed after me.

One of the special aspects of playing professional tennis is becoming a part of an international community that travels the world together. As the tennis tour grew, it became commonplace that no matter where you came from, no matter what your background — race, religion, citizenship— once you arrived on the tour you were respected as someone who belonged. The world might not be that open-minded, even today, but the tennis circuit has proven itself to be color blind and religiously accepting.

I grew up in a time when individual sports such as tennis and golf were formerly considered country club pursuits, but were breaking out to mainstream popularity. Kids saw players at the country club, or the public park, with tennis racket in hand, hitting tennis balls over a net. It looked like fun, and more and more wanted to try playing themselves.

With tennis earning more universal appeal, it's not surprising that I was one of quite a number of Jewish players who came to the pro ranks at the same time. Prior to my generation, there were definitely Jewish players on the tour, but certainly not as many playing at the same time.

I have to say that I never really thought much about the Jewish players and their stories as something to package in a book, maybe because I'm not a writer. I guess I just saw everyone as who they were without necessarily knowing what helped make them that way.

When Sandy called me early in the summer of 2013 to tell me of the book she was writing I was interested to hear about it, and I was happy for her to interview me for the book. I've known Sandy for a very long time. She joined the tour as a sportswriter in 1979 and being that it was a different time in those days, there wasn't the mentality that you're a writer, I'm a player and we need to keep a distance from each other. In those days, at the advent of pro tennis, the players knew we would benefit from promoting ourselves and the game. And a writer who knew the game as well as Sandy could help us push the cause. In the big picture, that meant that everybody who had an essential role on the tour was considered to be a part of the tennis family.

Sandy came down to see me at the Harold Solomon Tennis Institute, where we spent some time catching up and discussing some of the players she'd already talked to and those she still planned to speak to for the book. I wondered about how many players she had identified and also started throwing out names.

In early 2014, Sandy called again. She was nearly done with the writing and sounded really happy with how it was all turning out. After agreeing to write the foreword to the book, she sent me a few of the chapters and I read them over. I told Sandy a few days later I loved what I read and can't wait to see what she uncovered about other players in the rest of her book. As I read what she sent along, I quickly realized that all of us players that shared a Jewish background did so in very diverse ways. The fact that we were all Jewish was a reason to group us together under the same book cover, but we were all very unique individuals. Some of the players Sandy wrote about I had never heard of — Umberto Louis de Morpurgo comes to mind. Others, I knew of them, but not much about their story. And then there were people I knew fairly well but discovered that Sandy's research had dug up some interesting facts about them that weren't common knowledge.

I think this is a book that will appeal to a wide variety of readers. Obviously, tennis and sports fans will enjoy the read. Obviously, those of the Jewish faith will be interested in reading about successful Jewish athletes at the highest level of a sport. One thing is for sure, however, you don't need to be Jewish to appreciate the story of any of these Jewish tennis players. You just have to be someone who has a curious side and likes to learn about people and how they ended up being who they are and doing what they did.

ACKNOWLEDGEMENTS

I've actually had great trepidation thinking about writing the acknowledgements for this book. This is my first published title — hopefully not my last — and I worried about including everyone who should be mentioned. So let me say at the outset if I happened to omit you, it was just a terrible oversight and I really did mean to include you in this list of thanks.

I want to thank the players — past and present — who took the time to talk with me for this book as I couldn't have written it without your generous input: Elise Burgin, Angela Buxton, Pierre Darmon, Jonathan Erlich, Allen Fox, Noam Gershony, Brad Gilbert, Justin Gimelstob, Brian Gottfried, Julia Glushko, Jim Grabb, Aaron Krickstein, Jesse Levine, Scott Lipsky, Amos Mansdort, Shahar Pe'er, Andy Ram, Dick Savitt, Harold Solomon, and Brian Teacher.

And I want to thank all the players who have offered their thoughts, comments, and friendship from my first assignment covering tennis to my most recent article. Without all of your cooperation I wouldn't have had as much fun following you around the world while you chased the fuzzy yellow ball.

I also must thank all the public relations people who have helped make me feel at home wherever I turned up on a given week. This book wouldn't have been possible without the help from all my special friends in the communication departments at the alphabets — ITF, ATP, WTA and USTA. There are a few people I need to thank in particular: Barbara Travers, my great friend of nearly 30 years, who came up with contact information and other help through the research and writing process. Barbara, on more than one occasion, also offered her Brentford, England, home as a temporary home base for me to hang my hat and spend hours writing this book. I'd like to thank the fabulous Nick Imison, who is the General of Interviews — and I mean General in a loving military precision way — at all the majors except for Wimbledon. He made many of the interviews for this book happen and was dogged about doing so. Also many thanks to Nicola Arzani and Greg Sharko who put me in touch with a number of people and checked in on occasion to see how the book was coming along. And a big thanks to Eloise Tyson, a great go-between, who also helped in organizing interviews and inquired to make sure they took place.

There are so many of my colleagues who have been a part of my life as a journalist, offering their friendship, encouragement, willingness to debate, crucial work assignments, etc., all of which helped me through the writing of this book. They are listed here in no particular order: Matt Wilansky, Howard Fendrich, Steve Wilson, John Pye, Chuck Culpepper, Alix Ramsay, Eleanor Preston, Liza Horan, Bud Collins and wife, Anita Klaussen, Ashley Brown, Peter Bodo, Mark Preston, Sally Milano, Harvey Fialkov, Jorge Rojas, Alex Mena, Linda

Robertson, Walter Villa, Liz Clarke, Christopher Clarey, Doug Robson, Matt Cronin, Joel Drucker, Donna Doherty, Richard Evans, Sebastien Fest, Paul Newman, Bill Simons, Jon Wertheim, Linda Pearce, Tom Perrotta, Eli Weinstein, Tom Tebbutt, Steve Flink, Paul Zimmer, Cynthia Lum and Cindy Shmerler.

I can't thank enough my longtime friend and fabulous editor, Janet Graham, who read behind me as I wrote — every last word down to the final day for manuscript submission. Her remarkable light editing touch and critical eye to detail definitely enhanced the stories on the pages ahead. Interestingly, it was my artistic talent and not my writing ability that first bonded us in friendship — yes, this is an inside story that only Janet will appreciate and I won't tell.

My cousin, Amy Hackmyer Wish, an attorney and active member of her Jewish community in Maryland, also read behind me, offering a few key adjustments to make the Jewish information in the book clearer and more accurate.

I can't say enough about working with New Chapter Press. Randy Walker picked up on the fact that there was a book in the Jewish tennis players through the years and was thankfully keen to have me do the writing. Yes, I know I was a bit slow in getting it done — a perfectionist personality tends to get in the way — but it was so easy and fabulous to work with Randy as my point person, especially his patience as I kept pushing the deadline back.

A shout-out to a special group of people who have been there like family, especially in the past few years when their encouragement was essential: Richard Bush, Marilyn and Frank Marcellino, Judy and Harry Isaacs, Michelle

Kaufman and Dave Barry, Susan and Fred Mullane, Barbara Travers, Craig Gabriel, the entire Degnan family (Susan, Kevin, Meredith, Ellen, Bernie and Susan's mom, Millie), Robin and the late great Francois Padial, Janet Graham, Laura Ostheimer, Debbie Ostheimer, Cynthia and Steve Wine, Carol Cedar, Prajwal Hegde, Diane Pucin, Gwen Shusterman, and Robin Serody.

My sister, Cathy offered the greatest gift in Michael and Alicia, my nephew and niece. They've offered their encouragement throughout the process of writing this book and the belief that I could get it done when I wasn't so sure. And Michael, Alicia and now Alicia's husband, Kevin, have happily indulged a doting aunt in many special times and trips through the years.

During the writing of this book we sadly lost my dad, Ernie Harwitt, at age 92 in September 2013. He was a World War II hero, who overcame a battle with trench feet and gangrene to walk close to two miles a day until he was about 89. A man with advanced degrees, it was painful to see his decline the last few years from dementia. Before that last battle, his greatest hobbies were watching sports on TV and reading. Each time he closed a book for the final time he would often say the same thing, "This is the best book I've read," put in a well-timed momentary pause and then add the clincher, "this week." And he could definitely read more than one book a week. I can just imagine how proud he would've been to open a book written by his daughter and am hopeful that when he'd say, "This is the best book I've read," there wouldn't have been a ''this week'' attached to the end of his thought.

And finally, my mom, who has always been very support-ive in whatever adventures I have pursued. She has been a best friend and introduced me to the privileges of being a native New Yorker — the museums, theater, shops, restau-rants — all of which she started showing me as a very little girl. It didn't matter that when I was 5 I thought the circular-designed Guggenheim museum was the best skipping place in the world, or that after months of hearing that we were going to see the Mona Lisa, the most important painting in the world, and my reaction was a loud pronouncement, "That's it — it's so small," we kept going until I developed an appreciation for what I was seeing. Although I must admit that I still agree with my original opinion that the Mona Lisa is small. Into her mid-80s, my mother remains a lifelong avid reader and her Kindle is never too far away. I hope she will read this book — hopefully as an old-fashioned page turner instead of on her Kindle — not only for herself but for my dad, too.

Sandra Harwitt
June 2014

INTRODUCTION

It likely comes as no surprise that in today's world the idea for this book was generated from a Twitter feed. I must admit to not being the most dedicated of tweeters, but out of the necessity of the business, I make sure to check out what is going on a few times a day — and I even throw in an occasional tweet of my own.

So when I went on one day in the winter of 2013, my friend and colleague Joel Drucker and author Marshall Jon Fisher, who wrote the fabulous *A Terrible Splendor: Three Extraordinary Men, A World Poised For War, And The Greatest Tennis Match Ever Played* were engaging in a back-and-forth conversation as to who were the greatest Jewish players in the game – yesterday and today. I was just following along as the discussion eventually landed on who was the most successful Jewish man in the Open Era. Joel and Marshall decided the honor would either fall to Harold Solomon or Brian Gottfried, both of whom reached the French Open final a year apart in the mid-1970s. It was at this juncture that I inserted myself into the debate to say that if results at the majors were the determining factor, I had to disagree with them both. The clear winner would have to be Brian Teacher, who won the 1980 Australian Open title.

By this point, Randy Walker, formerly with the USTA public relations department, now an independent public relations consultant who also runs the publishing company New Chapter Press, started to get involved in the chat. Somewhere in there, he put out the thought that the topic would make a great book so who wanted to write it. I responded, half kiddingly, that I'd write it. The next thing you know Randy said he would call me the next day to discuss it, and soon a contract was signed, research was being done and stories were being crafted.

When word started to filter out that I was writing this book — or Randy would tell people he'd be publishing this title in the new year — the most frequent comment went something like this: "It's going to be a really small book?" "Is it a short story?" Or my favorite — "It must be a pamphlet."

As anyone can see from holding the book, that is far from the truth. In fact, I had little trouble identifying more than 70 players who fall into the category of Jewish professional tennis players, and while I tried to get everyone at least a mention, I will readily admit to having to choose who to profile.

And if you put the achievements of these world-class athletes all together you'll find that, combined, they won more than 180 official ATP or WTA singles titles and that's just the count in the Open Era.

The common thread in this project is that all the subjects are Jewish but this book is not a story of their Jewishness — for some it is a component in their story, for others not so much. But from the stories I already knew, to the stories I discovered in the digging I did, there were some incredibly interesting players with intriguing stories to tell. And, as an aside, they just so happen to all be Jewish.

My first step in the process of putting this book together was to search for all the details and information. I found many books that seemed as if they could be somewhat related to the subject at hand and went about purchasing them all. As anticipated, there was no book totally dedicated to tennis — mine would clearly be the first. But there were many others that could potentially be helpful and I'm quite sure that amazon.com appreciated my business. I'm not so sure the FedEx man enjoyed the heavy packages he had to deliver. Some of the books contained Jewish tennis players among their pages, others didn't, but they all had a purpose. From them, I pulled information, such as a player or two I never heard of before, as well as style ideas.

In one book, *The Big Book Of Jewish Sports Heroes: An Illustrated Compendium Of Sports History & The 150 Greatest Jewish Sports Stars* by Peter S. Horvitz, I was stunned to find the name of a very famous American who I neither knew of as a Jew or an athlete: Elvis Presley. As I read, it turned out that Elvis as an athlete was more of a stretch than Elvis as a Jew. Apparently, at least technically, Elvis' mother, Gladys Love Smith, was the daughter of Octavia Mansell, who was the daughter of Martha Tackett, a Jewess who lived from 1852 to 1887. In the eyes of traditional Jews, that makes Elvis completely Jewish since religion is inherited from your mother. According to Horvitz, Elvis was aware of his Jewish roots but was not raised in the faith. He also says that somewhere in Israel stands a statue of Elvis wearing a yarmulke on his head. From what I can tell, the Israelis are big Elvis fans — I can't say whether they just like his music or have heard he's, technically speaking, a landsman. Where the connection is fudged by Horvitz is calling Elvis an athlete — he participated in sports like any sport-minded person — that is true. But he doesn't appear to have credentials of competing at an elite level in any particular sport. He played high school football and participated in games on the army base where he was stationed in Germany when serving in the military. He was a black belt in karate. And he played sports figures in the movies: boxer Kid Galahad and a race car driver. Sadly, there was no mention that Elvis ever owned a tennis racket or played the game.

Initially, when I contemplated how this book would take shape, I envisioned a narrative intertwining the players together instead of handling each person as an individual. That was the approach I took — and took — and took. Eventually, I realized that approach was not only making things greatly complicated but it was actually diminishing each player's story. So I gave up that route — deleted it all — and started again. The second time around, I went in a direction that was simpler but worked. The words started to flow, the stories started to form their own personalities.

Unfortunately, there were only so many pages that this book could go — it was just one book, after all, not volumes. So I used my best judgment as to which stories to tell. While many might suggest I offer something on the Top 50 Jewish players, I actually decided to take my cue from the Hebrew word Chai, which translates to alive or living, something that all the subjects in this book did or are doing to the fullest.

Chai also translates to the number 18 in Gematria, a system of Jewish numerology and because of that decoding of Chai, 18 is considered a very lucky number to those of the Jewish faith. In fact, Jewish people often give gifts (money most notably) in multiples of 18. So in this book you might think I somehow ran out of players 14 short of the Top 50, but I consciously chose to give you the best of the best Jewish players via double Chai chapters.

In the end, I believe I've highlighted a blend of very different people that will entertain and inform the reader. At least that is what my intention and hopes were for *The Greatest Jewish Tennis Players Of All Time.*

WHO IS A JEW?

Choosing The Criteria For Inclusion In The Book

I've always had the notion of writing a book in my mind. It was just a case of finding the right project. Once that project was identified — telling the story of the incredibly talented Jewish tennis players who have made — or are making — an indelible mark on the sport, my next task was determining the ideal jumping-off point for this undertaking.

As I set about the research and interviewing process, I contemplated how best to give birth to *The Greatest Jewish Tennis Players Of All Time*. I reasoned with myself that this would be no different than how I approach writing an article, whether for a newspaper or magazine — find your lead and the rest will flow, even if this time, my work would have far greater depth and breadth. As I continued to consider the shaping of the book, I would, almost disturbingly, hear Julie Andrews singing in my head from *The Sound of Music*: "Let's Start At The Very Beginning, A Very Good Place To Start."

In truth, my vision never wavered. The place to start was with a simple question that came with anything but a simple answer: Who is a Jew?

Some might be chuckling right about now in their thinking a Jewish person is a Jewish person. What's so complicated? Ah, but leave it to the wonderful world of Judaism to allow for broad interpretation and great debate regarding who is and who isn't a member of the tribe.

For starters, formally speaking, there are a number of very distinct branches of Judaism: Orthodox, Conservadox, Conservative, Reform and Reconstructionist. Suffice it to say that while they all share a core belief in the Jewish religion, they all come with their own version of how to practice the faith. And all this doesn't take into account religiously non-practicing Jews, who nevertheless often have a strong Jewish identity from a cultural perspective.

All these different sects of Judaism hold varying opinions on many issues, including who exactly qualifies to be a Jew. It would pretty much take a book, as well as qualified rabbis and theological experts, to separate the beliefs of the different sects, but here's a brief overview.

The traditionalists adhere to the opinion that when it comes to determining who qualifies as a Jewish person the religion is a matriarchal society. That's something different from the day-to-day practice of Judaism and where you fall in the spectrum of Judaism, which is determined by a patrilineal order. For instance, there are 12 tribes of Israel that descend from Jacob — some are priestly and some are just plain regular folk. The tribe a Jewish person belongs to is the tribe of their father.

Now, of course, there are many Jews who aren't all that immersed into the religion. I tend to be one of those non-sectarian types. I have no idea what tribe I descended from and if I had to guess, I wouldn't be so sure my dad, Ernie, would've had the answer either. So as I wrote this, I decided to give my first cousin, Roberta Harwitt Shoten, a call and ask her whether she knew. She was better than I was, as she thought we were Israelites, but admitted she wasn't totally sure.

But, obviously, before you can be a member of a tribe you have to know you're a Jew. According to Jewish law (Halacha) a person is Jewish if they were born to a Jewish mother, but not a Jew if born to a non-Jewish mother even if one's father is Jewish. In truth, there is nothing specifically written in the Torah that formally states this fact. Instead, Jewish scholars point to clues scattered within the Hebrew Bible to support the opinion that Judaism is a matrilineal inheritance.

Deuteronomy 7: 1-5 talks against intermarriage with non-Jews:

3) Neither shalt thou make marriages with them; thy daughter thou shalt not give unto his son, nor his daughter shalt thou take unto thy son.

4) For they will turn away thy son from following me, that they may serve other gods: so will the anger of the LORD be kindled against you, and destroy thee suddenly.

Leviticus 24:10 calls the child of an Israelite woman and Egyptian man as being an Israelite:

10) Now the son of an Israelite woman, whose father was an Egyptian, went out among the sons of Israel; and the

Israelite woman's son and a man of Israel struggled with each other in the camp.

Ezra 10: 2-3 tells Jewish men returning to Israel not to bring their non-Jewish spouses and children with them:

2) We have trespassed against our God, and have taken strange wives of the people of the land: yet now there is hope in Israel concerning this thing.

3) Now therefore let us make a covenant with our God to put away all the wives, and such as are born of them, according to the counsel of my lord, and of those that tremble at the commandment of our God; and let it be done according to the law.

The Orthodox and more traditional believers take these missives strictly and believe that a child of a Jewish father with a non-Jewish mother cannot be a Jew without a conversion. They also believe a child of a Jewish mother, regardless if that child is brought up as a Jew, is a Jew.

The more liberal Jewish believers, such as adherents to Reform Judaism, are happy to welcome a child into their fold if either parent is Jewish, emphasizing that being raised in the Jewish faith is the integral ingredient to being considered a Jew.

In order to write this book I had to make a judgment as to which players can be included within the pages of *The Greatest Jewish Tennis Players Of All Time*. I've decided to focus on those players who were raised in the Jewish faith whether it be that their mother, father or both parents are Jewish. Not to do so would discount some players who definitely identify as Jewish, such as the "Flying Dutchman" Tom Okker, a former top 10 singles player and the 1976 U.S.

Open doubles champion. However, there will be some mention, but not a great deal of concentration, on some players who acknowledge a Jewish heritage or are known to have some Jewish background although they are not practicing Jews.

THE JEWISH BARON
Baron Umberto Louis De Morpurgo

In its initial incarnation, tennis was a sport for the elite, so it should come as no surprise that one of the first notable, internationally-known, Jewish tennis players was a titled gentleman.

Baron Hubert Luis de Morpurgo, who later would become known as Umberto instead of Hubert, was born into a patrician family on January 12, 1896. At the time, Trieste flew under the Austro-Hungarian flag, but following World War I, in which Hubert served in the German Air Force, Trieste changed hands and became part of Italy. That's when Hubert became an Italian citizen and changed from Hubert to Umberto.

The Morpurgo genealogy can be traced all the way back to Rabbi Israel Isserlein (1390-1460) who chose Marburg, Styria — now Maribor, Slovenia — as his home. In the 1600s, the family spread throughout Europe, and even into North Africa, and soon settled down in Trieste as well.

Establishing themselves in various professions of note, Emperor Ferdinand II of Austria bestowed upon the family the infrequent honor of being selected Jews of the Court.

Considering his noble heritage, it was appropriate that De Morpurgo spent some time being educated in England and became interested in tennis.

As a player, the Baron was a right-hander noted for a kick serve and all-around game. What he was less admired for was his inability to totally concentrate on tennis. Nevertheless, Umberto put together an impressive career when he did put his best effort into the time he spent on court.

Often referred to as Italy's Bill Tilden, De Morpurgo was the top player from his country in 1927, and then again between 1929 and 1931. On a more international scope, the Baron was considered a Top Ten player, and Tilden, who formulated his own world rankings each year, placed Umberto at No. 6 in 1929.

A Wimbledon quarterfinalist in 1928 and French semifinalist in 1930, the Baron was a Wimbledon mixed doubles finalist with Liz Ryan in 1925 and won the Italian National Championships mixed doubles title with Lili Alvarez in 1930.

There's no denying that Umberto's special moment in time came during the 1924 Olympics held in Paris. He disappointed local fans by ending Jean Borotra's hopes of an Olympic medal, defeating the reigning Wimbledon champion to capture the bronze medal.

Another highlight for Umberto in tennis was participating in the Davis Cup. He played on the first-ever Davis Cup squad for Italy when it joined the competition in 1922, and continued to represent the country every year through 1933. His Davis Cup efforts saw De Morpurgo amass a 39-14 singles and 16-10 doubles record.

In 1929, Benito Mussolini, who founded Italy's National Fascist Party and was the de facto dictator of Italy from 1922 through 1943, appointed De Morpurgo to the role of Italian Commissioner of Tennis.

Baron Umberto Louis De Morpurgo

Fleshing out the story of Umberto De Morpurgo isn't all that easy without a sound command of Italian. As for my knowledge of the language, it extends no further than knowing to answer the phone Pronto and saying Ciao when departing; to ordering lasagna and cannelloni, and even more importantly, asking for a refreshing glass of Prosecco or an after-dinner Limoncello.

So at Wimbledon 2013, I took advantage of the fact that Italian journalist Gianni Clerici, just weeks away from his 83rd birthday, moved his seat in the press room right next to mine, claiming the natives in the row he was assigned to were way too noisy for him to concentrate. A longtime author, reporter and broadcaster, Clerici, who was inducted into the International Tennis Hall of Fame in the contributor category in 2006, would likely have thoughts to express on Italy's famous tennis-playing Baron.

"Umberto De Morpurgo has been, perhaps, the best Italian player of all times except besides (Nicola) Pietrangeli," Clerici said. "He is from a family that was part of the Hapsburg Empire, but then Trieste became part of Italy so he became Italian too. Trieste was a piece of Italian history that was very mixed up. He started to play tennis when he was younger when he was in England. He was the best of the Italian team that reached the Inter-Zonal final of Davis Cup a couple of times.

"What can I say? Umberto had always been a very gentle person. He was from the time when tennis was just for the aristocrats. Of course, I met him one time when Italy was playing Davis Cup and he showed up. I was about 20 years old and he was already 80 so it wasn't a great conversation."

When asked whether he thought that De Morpurgo's Jewish background was ever a difficulty for him in Italy, Clerici quickly answered: "No, no, no. To be Jewish was not a problem. I am half-Jewish myself from my mother's side. (Clerici laughed when I suggested according to Jewish law he'd be considered fully Jewish with his mother being Jewish). In truth, I didn't even know he was Jewish at first because the problem with being Jewish didn't come until 1938, '39, when Hitler was influencing very much Mussolini. Mussolini was just sort of a prisoner of Hitler in the last years of his life, so then this was a problem in Italy. But there was not a problem for three or four centuries about being Jewish."

Umberto Louis De Morpurgo passed away in Geneva on February 26, 1961. In 1993, the Baron was posthumously elected to the International Jewish Sports Hall of Fame.

BEING EUROPE'S BEST MEANT NOTHING TO HITLER

Daniel Prenn

When it came to men's tennis in the early 1930s, all seemed to be in agreement that the Eastern European-born German Daniel Prenn was the preeminent player in the game. He had proudly represented Germany in Davis Cup on 31 occasions and played as a German at other international events. But despite his prominence as an exceedingly talented tennis player, in 1933 he was expelled from his Berlin tennis club and told he no longer was needed to compete in Davis Cup.

The reason: He was a Jew and certainly didn't fit the Aryan profile extolled by Adolf Hitler, who clearly disregarded the non-Aryan looking person who stared back at him from a mirror each morning. It was April 1933 and the German Tennis Federation released the statement that "no Jew may be selected for a national team or for the Davis Cup. No Jewish (or Marxist) club or association may be affiliated with the German Tennis Federation. No Jew may hold an official position in the Federation." And as Peter S. Horvitz wrote in *The Big Book Of Jewish Sports Heroes* "And, in case Daniel Prenn did not get the point, they added, 'The player Dr. Prenn (a Jew) will not be selected for the Davis Cup team in 1933.' "

Prenn, who was abroad at the time, received a telegram from the Reichssportfuhrer telling him his service was no longer required for Davis Cup and that he should return immediately to Germany. He smartly ignored the order to come home to Germany as world headlines reported that the Jewish player Daniel Prenn was being kept off the German Davis Cup squad.

On April 11, 1933, the Associated Press bureau in Berlin released the following news item regarding Prenn:

> *The Davis Cup hopes of Germany today were wrecked by the Hitler government's ban on Jews as the cup committee dropped its leading player and former captain Daniel Prenn, because of his race.*

> *The disbarment left Germany with only Baron Von Cramm to renew the campaign which twice in four years had carried her to the inter-zone final against the United States. The third and fourth ranking players — G. Jaenecke and E Nourney — are not considered in the same class with the baron and Prenn.*

> *Germany faced a difficult Davis Cup campaign even with Prenn being drawn in the lower half of the European zone with Japan, Ireland, Australia and South America. Without him they face almost certain elimination.*

Prenn has been Germany's leading player for several years and in 1932 was one of the 10 or 15 best in the world. He first headed the German list in 1928, repeated in 1929 and and 1930 and in 1931 shared the place with Von Cramm. He again was ranked No. 1 in 1932.

Experiencing anti-Semitism was definitely not a new phenomenon for Prenn. Through-out his life, he'd been sub-jected to worries stemming from his being a Jew.

Life began for Prenn on September 7, 1904. Some histor-ical accounts say he was born in Poland; others suggest the birth was in Vilnius, now a city in Lithuania but at the time part of Russia. His family went on to live in St. Petersburg and while considered a more broad-minded city in Russia, there were still regulations in place for what Jews could and couldn't do. Life under the Czarist system was not favorable to Jews and many met their demise in bloody pogroms. The Russian Revolution didn't improve the lot of Jews in Russia either, and, along with many other Russian Jewish families, the Prenns chose emigration in the hopes of a more posi-tive future. They fled to Berlin, arriving in the cosmopolitan German city in 1920.

The teenage Daniel took well to Germany and flourished in school, eventually going on to procure a doctorate degree in engineering. He also was successful playing a variety of sports. But it was tennis that seemed to be in perfect har-mony with Prenn's natural fierce competitive instinct — he might not have been known as a suave and power player, but the words "give up" didn't exist in his vocabulary. It's a good thing that his style of play relied on a tireless defense to wear out opponents.

In the book *Emancipation Through Muscles: Jews and Sports in Europe*, Prenn is quoted from an interview given to the C.V. Zeitung that related the success of "Jewish sportsmen" to Jewish oppression resulting in a "combative" aggression, which seemed incongruous to the normal impression that Jewish people tended toward taking a gentle posture. Prenn responded: "That is only an apparent contradiction, for having pacifist convictions can certainly go hand in hand with the enjoyment of competitive contact sport."

Daniel Prenn

Prior to Prenn being banned from competition, he was the top German tennis star, and in 1929 led the German team to a surprise win over Great Britain in the Davis Cup European final held at the Rot-Weiss Club where he played. Prenn would deliver the tie victory in the decisive fifth rubber, beating an exhausted Bunny Austin, who, down 1-5, 0-30 in the final set, retired with cramps. The euphoria from toppling Great Britain was brief as the following week the United States, armed with the incomparable 36-year-old Bill Tilden, scored a flawless 5-0 Inter-Zone round win over Germany, also held at the Rot-Weiss Club.

It would not be Prenn's sole success in Davis Cup. Germany would again beat Great Britain in the 1932 European semifinals. Prenn and good friend, Baron

Gottfried von Cramm, would square off against Fred Perry and Austin. From there, Germany would defeat Italy in the European Zone final before losing to the United States in the Inter-Zone final held at Stade Roland Garros in Paris.

Those achievements saw many exulting Prenn as a German tennis hero, but the good times were not going to last. Germany was in turmoil. Financially, it was a country in trouble, a situation that often leads to public dissatisfaction. As had happened in the past, certainly to the Prenn family when in Russia, it was the Jewish people who were primed as the scapegoat for all that was wrong.

In 1933, Prenn would be personally touched by the anti-Semitism overtaking Germany. Despite being the lifeline of German tennis, Daniel might be needed but wasn't wanted. As Marshall Jon Fisher told in his remarkable tome, *A Terrible Splendor*, it didn't matter that Prenn was far from religious and his wife, Charlotte, was a Christian. And it didn't matter that a number of prominent people came to Prenn's defense — Sweden's King Gustav V made a not-so-subtle statement of support by playing doubles with Prenn at the Rot-Weiss Club during a visit to Germany in early 1933.

Fred Perry and Bunny Austin, who were on the 1932 Davis Cup team that lost to Prenn and Germany, took the matter of his Davis Cup exclusion to the media, penning a letter to the *London Times*:

> *Sir, We have read with considerable dismay the official statement which has appeared in the press that Dr. D. D. Prenn is not to represent Germany in the Davis Cup on the grounds that he is of Jewish origin. We cannot but recall the scene*

when, less than twelve months ago, Dr. Prenn before a large crowd at Berlin won for Germany against Great Britain the semifinal round of the European Zone of the Davis Cup, and was carried from the arena amidst spontaneous and tremendous enthusiasm. We have always valued our participation in international sport, because we believed it to be a great opportunity for the promotion of better international understanding and because it was a human activity that countenanced no distinction of race, class, or creed. For this reason, if for none other, we view with great misgivings any action which may well undermine all that is most valuable in international competitions.

Yours faithfully, H.W. Austin, Fred Perry

Aware that his future could no longer be in Germany, Prenn knew it was time again to move on. It was not his first time fleeing, but it would be the last time he'd have to relocate because of religious persecution. Having forged a friendship with Simon Marks, the Jewish retailer of Marks & Spencer department store fame, during his frequent visits to Wimbledon, Prenn relied on Marks as a benefactor in his move to England. Until Baron Gottfried von Cramm was jailed by the Nazis for refusing to join the Nazi Party — his being known as a homosexual didn't help his cause with the Party either — he would visit Prenn in England and funnel money to his old friend as well.

Once ensconced in Great Britain, Prenn's life dramatically changed as he went from being a tennis player to businessman. He would continue to play at Wimbledon through 1939, falling to John Olliff in the first round in his final All

England Club appearance as a competitor. But life was predominantly about building the Prenn family empire, to which he was very successful. He started with a company called Truvox that manufactured loudspeakers, and continued to acquire other companies as well. His entrepreneurial ways led to his acceptance into the luxurious world of a blue-blood British lifestyle.

It would take 51 years for Daniel Prenn, then 80 years old, to agree to a return visit to Germany, which included a visit to the Rot-Weiss Club. Nearly seven years later, in September 1991, Prenn, who had by then declined from Alzheimer's disease, passed away in his adopted homeland of Great Britain where his being Jewish held no adverse consequences. He was enshrined into the International Jewish Hall of Fame in 1981.

THE FIRST MACCABIAH GAMES
TENNIS CHAMPION
Ladislav Hecht

Born on August 31, 1909 in Zsolna, then a Hungarian city that is now called Zilina and part of Slovakia, Ladislav Hecht was not a child from a strong tennis family. In fact, his interest in tennis was self-developed when, as a curious 11-year-old, he picked up a tennis instructional manual and taught himself the game. Like many others around the world who came to the sport, Hecht learned his technique by employing a wall as his hitting partner.

Hecht obviously excelled at self-education, at least when it came to tennis, and developed into a top European competitor in the 1930s. He relied on a topspin forehand and backhand slice to keep opponents at bay. He would experience good fortune when taking on the likes of many well-known players of the time: Bobby Riggs, Fred Perry and Jack Crawford were among the players he claimed victories over. His best singles result at a major was, as the No. 7 seed, reaching the 1938 Wimbledon quarterfinals. In doubles, he reached the semifinals of the 1934 French Championships and 1937 Wimbledon events.

He excelled in playing Davis Cup for Czechoslovakia in the 1930s, playing in 18 ties from his first appearance in the international team competition in 1931. He put together an 18-19 Davis Cup record — 14-15 in singles and 4-4 in doubles. Interestingly, in 1938, around the time that Germany secured influence over Czechoslovakia, the Nazis apparently were unaware that Hecht was Jewish and proposed he should compete as part of the German Davis Cup team. Not surprisingly, he passed on the offer.

One of Hecht's most notable achievements was in winning the tennis title at the first Maccabiah Games — the Jewish Olympics — held in Tel Aviv, Israel in 1932.

As the 1930s moved on, Hecht could see that the political climate in Europe was no longer suitable and the continent was the wrong place for a Jew to be, so he started to weigh his options. In search of a new homeland, the December 14, 1938 edition of the *Canberra Times* reported in a very small item that Hecht was interested in the possibility of relocating to Australia:

Czech Tennis Star Seeks Job

If suitable employment can be found for him, Ladislav Hecht, who has represented Czechoslovakia in the Davis Cup, will come to Australia to live. This information was contained in a letter which the Present of the L.T.A. of Australia (Mr. Norman Brooks) received today from the President of the Czechoslovakian Tennis Association.

Mr. Brooks said that an endeavor would be made to secure a job for Hecht.

Hecht would get out of Europe just in time — three days before Germany invaded Czechoslovakia in 1939. But he would not be headed for Australia. He went west to the United States, choosing Kew Gardens, a comfortable community in the New York borough of Queens, to be the place he would call home for the rest of his life. During World War II, Ladislav would work in ammunition plants in New Jersey. After the war, he would continue to play tennis well into his senior days. And he would own a paintbrush and toy business.

Despite being forced to leave his homeland, the people of Slovakia never stopped considering Hecht as one of their own. In 1996, they named a multi-sport stadium in Bratislava in his honor and invited him to be there to witness the occasion. According to *The New York Times* obituary for Hecht written by Frank Litsky, Hecht's grandson Nikos said he didn't return to Slovakia to attend the ceremony because "he thought honors like that were unimportant."

Ladislav Hecht

Litsky's obit also contained the following sentence regarding Hecht: "In 1938, when Don Budge achieved a Grand Slam by winning the world's four major tournaments,

Hecht twice had him at match point at Wimbledon." That same information also appears on Hecht's bio page on the International Jewish Sports Hall of Fame.

Historical records, however, dispute the notion that Hecht had any match points on Budge at Wimbledon in 1938. In fact, the two did not play each other that year — they did face off in the 1937 Wimbledon draw with Budge winning their fourth-round meeting, 6-4, 6-2, 6-2. In 1938, Budge won Wimbledon with straight-set victories over Kenneth Gandon-Dower, Henry Billington, George Lyttleton-Rogers, Ronald Shayes, Frantisek Cejnar, Franjo Puncec, and Bunny Austin — not a Hecht in the crowd. Actually, Hecht's 1938 Wimbledon campaign ended in the quarterfinals to Henner Henkel after wins over Derrick Leyland, Jacques van den Eyndem, Nigel Sharpe, and Franjo Kukuljevic.

Hecht was 94 years old when, after a brief illness, he died at his home in Kew Gardens on May 27, 2004. The following year, he was posthumously inducted into the International Jewish Sports Hall of Fame.

THE JEWISH WOMAN'S GOAT - GREATEST OF ALL TIME
Zsuzsa (Suzy) Kormoczy

The search for the most accomplished Jewish woman to play tennis requires some heavy research. But persistence often pays off as it did on this occasion with the discovery that the late Hungarian player Zsuza Kormoczy qualifies as the top Jewish woman to ever play the game. What enables Kormoczy to win the nod is her status as the winner of the 1958 French Championships, making Hungary's 1958 Sportswoman of the Year the only Jewish woman to date to win one of the four most coveted singles trophies in tennis.

Suzy Kormoczy is barely on the tip of anyone's tongue. Most have never heard of the tennis talent and finding information about the Hungarian — there doesn't seem to be much of an offering in Hungarian no less English — is a challenge.

Born on August 25, 1924, Kormoczy is the pride and joy of Hungarian tennis. While other Hungarians might be more familiar to tennis fans — Andrea Temesvari and Balazs Taroczy come to mind — it is "Suzy K" who is the country's greatest success story.

By 1939, Kormoczy was traveling abroad and had the opportunity to meet tennis idols from America — Bill Tilden and Alice Marble — when at Wimbledon. She asked Marble, who would win the Wimbledon title that year with a 6-2, 6-0 win over Briton Kay Stammers, for an autograph. Marble wrote, "To Suzy, I hope you will someday win Wimbledon, Alice Marble."

Suzy Kormoczy

Kormoczy would never win Wimbledon — clay and not grass was her surface of choice — but she would come fairly close. The petite Hungarian would reach the Wimbledon semifinals in 1958, just weeks after winning the French title, and the quarterfinals in 1953 and 1955.

A resilient baseliner, the terre battue at Roland Garros and at other European events, was where Kormoczy performed to high standards. In 1958, following rigorous pre-Roland Garros training that included running and gymnastics, Kormoczy, at the ripe old age of 33, earned her place in history. She captured the French National crown with a 6-4, 1-6, 6-2 victory over Shirley Bloomer Brasher of Britain, becoming the oldest ever French champion, a distinction she still holds. Following behind Kormoczy as the next oldest French champions are Serena Williams (2013): 31 years, 8 months, Nelly Adamson-Landry (1948): 31 years and 6 months, and Chris Evert (1986): 31 years and 5 months.

As the defending champion in 1959, Kormoczy returned to the final, but couldn't hoist the trophy again. She lost out to 18-year-old Englishwoman Christine Truman 6-4, 7-5, who became the youngest ever French women's champion until she lost that honor to a 17-year-old Steffi Graf in 1987.

Although formal rankings were still decades away, sports journalists would take to ranking players on their own. And in 1958, when Kormoczy won eight of the nine tournaments she entered, losing in the Wimbledon semifinal to Briton Angela Mortimer 6-0, 6-1, it appeared unanimous that Kormoczy would occupy the No. 2 spot. At home, she was feted with the first-ever Hungarian Sportswoman of the Year award in honor of her incredible 1958 season.

In Hungary, she would win the national singles title six times, and the doubles or mixed doubles trophies on 10 occasions. She first won at home as a 16-year-old in 1940, taking the doubles and mixed doubles title.

From what is known, Kormoczy suffered with kidney stones throughout her career, which disrupted her ability to play at times. Following her career as a player, Kormoczy would become a coach at Vasas, her club, and the manager of the National Tennis Association.

Kormoczy passed away at age 82 on September 16, 2006. Tributes calling attention to her incredible life were offered by a number of players who followed her footsteps into professional tennis. Andrea Temesvari said, "This is a huge loss for the Hungarian tennis life. She belonged to the all-time greats." Balazs Taroczy said, "The tennis and her family were her life. She loved her club, "Vasas" where I also played. I'm sorry for not being able to watch her play, but I know she was a big fighter, a wonderful player, and a great person."

In 2007, Zsuzsa Kormoczy was posthumously inducted into the International Jewish Sports Hall of Fame.

THE JEWISH MEN'S GOAT - GREATEST OF ALL TIME

Richard "Dick" Savitt

It's likely that not everyone at the Morgan Stanley offices in Manhattan is aware their distinguished 86-year-old colleague Richard "Dick" Savitt had a previous career that brought him fame, if not fortune.

Indeed, when Savitt, a self-taught tennis player, was in his 20s, he was a world-class tennis champion. How famous was he? Let's put it this way — following his capturing of the 1951 Australian men's singles title, he achieved the greatest goal in tennis by reigning victorious at Wimbledon that same year. At home, *Time* magazine feted Savitt as they would any superstar by honoring him with the cover of the magazine. It was Savitt's first time gracing the grass courts at the All England Club and he remains the last man to capture the coveted Wimbledon trophy on his first attempt.

Savitt's success at those two majors also wrote a new page of Jewish history — he became the first person of the Jewish faith to score a singles trophy at any major. Since Savitt, only one other player who considers themselves purely Jewish has won a singles title at one of the four major — American Brian Teacher, who followed in Savitt's footsteps in winning the 1980 Australian Open title. There are, however, two other former No. 1 players in possession of multiple titles at the majors who can trace their family lineage to include a Jewish heritage: Boris Becker, whose mother is from a Jewish background, and Pete Sampras, whose paternal grandmother was Jewish. But speaking of full Jewish credit for a man winning a singles title at a major, it's all about Savitt and Teacher.

Life for Savitt began in Bayonne, New Jersey, and through his high school years he lived life as a native of the Garden State, moving on to Maplewood in the first year of his life, and eventually to South Orange when he was 13. A lover of all sports, tennis wasn't even initially on the radar for Savitt, who pursued basketball and baseball with a passion. Once in South Orange, Savitt incorporated a bit of self-taught tennis into his sports routine and that's when someone took notice of the kid on court at the public park. That someone was a member of the family who owned the drugstore in town, who also happened to be a member of the Berkeley Tennis Club in Orange, New Jersey. Savitt accepted an invitation from the gentleman to visit Berkeley and was quickly taken with the place. Berkeley was a great breeding ground for junior players and ex-collegiate stars, and the club president, Russell Kingman, happened to also be the current president of the United States Lawn Tennis Association.

"So between all the players and ex-college players and the juniors that were around (Berkeley) it was a whole other world for me — I'd never seen or been involved in a tennis situation like that," Savitt remembers. "In June, they held the New Jersey State Championships, and because Kingman was involved, Jack Kramer, Ted Schroeder, Pancho Segura, Bobby Riggs, all the great players of that time came to the New Jersey State and I got hooked. I was a ball boy and that's how I got into tennis."

Although he attended his first year of high school in South Orange, the Savitt family would soon move out of state.

"My parents moved to El Paso, Texas," Savitt said. "My mother had a bad skin condition and needed the warmer weather. My senior year in high school I was second all-team in basketball." Asked whether the adjustment to Texas was tough for a Jewish kid from New Jersey, no less a teen who grew up a stone's throw away from New

Dick Savitt

York City, Savitt quickly dispelled the suggestion. Savitt and El Paso went together as well as a horse and carriage: "Texas is great for high school sports — all sports — football, high school basketball. The weather was great and I could play tennis all year round and I would've never been able to play that much in New Jersey, obviously on account of the weather."

While at El Paso High School, Dick would play forward on the basketball team and was named to the Texas Second Team All-State basketball team. In tennis, he became the

Texas State junior tennis champ. He was then ranked No. 4 in the nation in the under-18s. Graduating high school in 1945, he joined the U.S. Navy and was stationed at the Naval Air Station in Memphis, Tennessee. World War II was coming to a close so during the winter of 1945-46 that he served in the Navy, he played on one of the top-ranked armed forces basketball teams. "A few months after I joined the Navy, the war ended," Savitt said. "I was still in the Navy for a year and a half but didn't go into battle. But if they hadn't dropped the bomb (on Hiroshima) I probably would've."

From the Navy in Memphis, Dick moved on in 1946 to college at Cornell, a school located "high above Cayuga's waters" in Ithaca, New York, as his alma mater's official song praises their upstate locale. A knee injury put an end to Savitt's collegiate basketball career, but he continued playing tennis, and won the Eastern Intercollegiate Tennis Tournament held in Syracuse, New York from 1947 through 1950.

Graduating from Cornell in 1950, Dick dedicated himself to tennis. That year, he won a number of tournaments, was considered the No. 6 ranked player in the country, and would reach the U.S. National semifinals at the West Side Tennis Club in Forest Hills. It was not, however, the first time he would play at the then grandest tennis stadium in the United States — he first gave it a go in 1947. In the first round that year, Savitt played against the renowned Bill Talbert, a 1944 and '46 U.S. National finalist. Savitt clearly remembers that first time playing at Forest Hills: "The place was packed to see Billy Talbert. The match was very quick and I think by the time I lost, even my parents had left the stadium. I guess I got off the court pretty quick because by the time Billy got to the clubhouse I was showered and dressed to leave. You've never seen anyone get dressed so fast. Playing in front of 14,000 was difficult."

It was in 1951 that Savitt utilized his tough-as-nails game — he overpowered opponents with potent groundstrokes and wicked serves — to indelibly link his name to the greats of the game. He would head down to Australia in January where he became the first non-Australian to win the Down Under major since American Don Budge in 1938.

"You need luck in life," Savitt said. "I had a friend who was No. 1 in Chile and I was invited to play in South America. I was in Chile and I got a wire while there from the USLTA asking if I wanted to go to Australia. It was meant to be Art Larsen and Herbie Flam, but Flam couldn't go because he was taking some courses at UCLA. So they asked me and I canceled the rest of the trip to South America and flew back and went to Australia with Larsen.

"I was playing full-time in Australia I really improved," Savitt added. "I was getting a lot of practice since there were so many courts. I beat (John) Bromwich, Frank Sedgman and Ken McGregor three days in a row so that was huge, especially beating Frank Sedgman in the semifinals since he was the best player in the world. It was a great win for me."

If Australia counts as a great win, Wimbledon remains the ultimate triumph in the sport. And Savitt was only months away from realizing that dream.

At Wimbledon, he defeated Herb Flam, his Davis Cup teammate — and a fellow Jewish player — in the semifinals.

And again, he would be staring across the net from McGregor in the final of a major — and like the last time in Australia, Dick was victorious, although this time in straight sets instead of four. *The New York Times* would declare Savitt the best amateur in the world — until the late '60s tennis was predominantly an amateur affair and the few barnstorming pros were not invited to play at the four majors or other prestigious events.

"It's probably the tournament to win — the major to win," said Savitt. "If you have to win just one, then Wimbledon is the one to win. It's got all the atmosphere. The other three majors are great tournaments, but I guess Wimbledon will always have a little bit of an edge."

Wimbledon in 1951 was the high of all highs for Savitt, but things were about to change.

He was considered the odds-on favorite at Forest Hills, but a leg infection would eventually take its toll and he lost to Vic Seixas in the semifinals.

In the year that would be his best, the Davis Cup would prove to deliver Savitt's biggest disappointment, and not because he was responsible for an American defeat. Dick was chosen to play during the early Davis Cup ties in 1951, compiling a 3-0 singles record in playing against Canada and Japan — those would turn out to be Dick's only career Davis Cup appearances. That's because when it came to the semifinals against Sweden and then the final against Australia, Dick didn't receive the nod. This seemed surprising since Savitt was universally considered the best player in the world at the time. Frank Shields — the grandfather to actress Brooke Shields — was the U.S. Davis Cup captain, and Jack Kramer was the coach — and they elected to play the semi-retired Ted Schroeder instead of Savitt. Schroeder was a close friend and former doubles partner of Kramer's, and as they often say, it's who you know. Schroeder would lose his matches, and the Australians would win the 1951 Davis Cup title.

To this day, it's easy to tell that not being named to the 1951 U.S. Davis Cup final team still smarts as if it was yesterday with Savitt: "Oh, you had to bring that up, didn't you?" Savitt asked, even though he knew it was going to be a topic of conversation. "I assumed I was going to play against the Australian team, but then came the announcement. The answer is, 'Yes, that was a low blow.'"

The rumor mill churned with many theories why Savitt was passed over for Schroeder. The assumption by many, especially Jewish tennis fans, was that Savitt being denied a place on the final squad was the doing of anti-Semitism, even though both Savitt and Flam took part in earlier rounds that year. Although many still are of the opinion that anti-Semitism sparked this Davis Cup incident, Savitt has never subscribed to that theory. He said, however, he never received a reason for why he was not selected. "There was no connection to anti-Semitism, I don't think," Savitt emphasized. "All the Jewish people weren't happy to know that, but I really don't think that was it." Savitt leaves it to "just that it was a bad time for me." And if anyone thinks that Savitt is just glossing over anti-Semitic overtones to this controversy, think again. He is a very open, direct and honest individual and if he thought for one minute that his being Jewish had anything to do with the Davis Cup snub, he'd say it loud and clear.

As it would turn out, Dick's day of playing tennis full-time were coming to a close. He would only play for one more season — the acclaim of being a tennis champion came without any ability to earn a living, which today's superstars enjoy. So in October 1952, Savitt announced his retirement with immediate plans of going out and getting a real job.

"Tennis in those days was different," Savitt said, noting his tennis never delivered an honest paycheck. "I didn't retire because of the Davis Cup. I retired because I only had two choices: to play as an amateur and receive money under the table as an appearance fee or teach tennis at a country club. I didn't want to do that. So I left to go into business."

Savitt initially went into the oil business in Texas and Louisiana, but after nine years would switch gears and go into securities on Wall Street: "Yeah, I've been here since 1961 until now," said Savitt, from his office. "These days I don't go in too early and I don't stay too late."

As he was in tennis, Savitt would be a success in the business world, too — and that included financial gain as well. But he didn't totally abandon playing tennis. He would continue to play at a competitive level, occasionally joining the draw of top tournaments in the Tri-State area. And even today, he still takes to the court for fun and exercise. "I get dressed three or four times a week, but what I play is not really tennis anymore," Savitt admitted. Although he went to Cornell University, it was another Ivy League school — Columbia University in Manhattan — where he has frequently played and helped with their team since 1972, which resulted in Columbia naming their tennis facility after him. One of his favorite trophies earned in his later years came when he teamed with his son, Robert, to win the 1981 USTA National Father-Son Indoor Championship.

Another tennis highlight of his life came in 1961 when he was changing the course of his career from oil to the stock market. Savitt made his first trip to Israel that year to play in the Maccabiah Games, winning the singles and doubles titles. It would be the beginning of a lifelong commitment to the Jewish homeland: "I'm very Israeli oriented," said Savitt, who made about 30 trips to Israel starting in the early 1970s, often going twice a year. Although he no longer travels on such long-haul voyages, he remains heavily dedicated to the Israel Tennis Centers efforts: "We now have 14 tennis centers and have had some great results as far as tournament players, Davis Cup players, Fed Cup players, and juniors," he said, proudly. "The major interest of the Israel Tennis Centers today is to keep all kinds of kids, not just Jewish kids, off the street. And we've succeeded in making Israel a tennis nation."

Savitt, who was elected to the Jewish Sports Hall of Fame in 1979, said he never experienced any anti-Semitism when playing tennis, although he was well aware that places like the West Side Tennis Club in Forest Hills didn't accept Jewish members: "I did play at clubs where I couldn't join, but I never thought about joining any of them and so I never had any problems." These days, of course, Savitt would be more than welcome to join the West Side Tennis Club, which now has members of all shapes, sizes, religions and races.

Savitt was enshrined into the International Tennis Hall of Fame in Newport, Rhode Island, in 1976.

THE FLIM FLAM MAN OF TENNIS
Herb Flam

In a *Village Voice* article *"The Dodgers: Triumph of the Nebbish"* by Stan Fischler that appeared on September 15, 1966, the author used Herb Flam as an example for why he was currently worried about the Los Angeles Dodgers, starting with their star pitcher, the Jewish Sandy Koufax. Fischler positioned his opinion tome by describing Flam as the retriever he was — he had no outstanding shots and his serve reportedly was recreational quality at best. But he was reliable at always getting to the ball and returning it, which served him well even if his serve didn't.

In the third paragraph of his article, Fischler wrote the following of Flam: "Herbie Flam, like the Dodgers, was born in Brooklyn and eventually emigrated to Los Angeles. Herbie developed into either the world's worst good tennis player or the world's best terrible tennis player. Probably the latter."

In the next two paragraphs Fischler continued chronicling Flam, saying, "Anyway, Herbie once won the Wimbledon championship and once he beat Pancho Gonzalez and once he was a finalist at Forest Hills, where he lost to Art Larsen, who was even more neurotic than Herbie. Few tennis players could make ANY of those statements. Few homo sapiens could either! "

There was only one problem with Fischler's information — he had something very wrong. Flam never was a Wimbledon champion because he never achieved any Grand Slam victories. But he certainly came close a couple of times. And the fact that Flam never won a major should not diminish his importance in tennis history.

Born in New York, Flam's family relocated to Southern California early on in his life. At age 10, he started playing tennis and two years later was winning junior tournaments. He attended UCLA, and in 1950, he not only led the school to its first-ever collegiate team title, but became the first Bruin to win the individual collegiate titles in singles and doubles.

Later in 1950, Flam introduced himself to the world on a grander stage when he became the first Jewish male player to reach the final of a major, doing so at the U.S. Championships, where he lost to Art Larsen 6-3, 4-6, 5-7, 6-4, 6-3. Back in those days, before there were official computer rankings, it was left to sportswriters and tennis publications to rank players. All were in immediate agreement that Herbie Flam belonged among the Top 10. Flam went on to reach one more career final at the Grand Slam level, at Roland Garros in 1957 where he lost in straight sets to Sven Davidson. He also reached the Australian semifinals in 1956.

Oh, and as for Wimbledon, Flam's best showing would've delighted many a player — he found a path to the semifinals in 1951 and 1952.

Flam won 20 career titles and was a Davis Cup stalwart, winning 12 of 14 matches played between 1951 and 1957.

After leaving the tennis big-time in 1963, Flam went back to Southern California, where he dabbled in a number of businesses and often gave private tennis lessons. A naval veteran who served in 1953

Herb Flam

and 1954, Flam had a troubled life later on and passed away at age 52 at a San Diego Veterans Hospital after an accident in which he was crippled.

Just bring up Herbie Flam's name to Ben Press and you can tell that he's smiling. Press, a San Diego native, fellow Bruin and Jew, went all the way back to the juniors with Herbie. Press, who spent much of his life as the head pro at the historic Hotel Del Coronado in San Diego, often played with Flam and also was a contemporary of players such as Jack Kramer, Bill Tilden, Bobby Riggs, Dick Savitt and Tony Trabert. Press didn't quite play to that level but he often played tournaments or just fun matches with Flam back "when I could still walk and chew gum," laughed Press. Press also was an important coach in San Diego and many of the best players from San Diego were students, including

Maureen Connolly, Karen Hantze Susman, Brian Teacher and Alexandra Stevenson.

Press laughed at some of his memories of Flam as he spoke to me while at the 2014 Qatar Total Open in Doha: "Do you have time for a Herbie story?" Press asked me. '"Sure," I replied. "I was so fond of Herbie. He was a great guy but he was a notorious bad driver. He was here in the Navy and he just kept getting ticket after ticket, and he finally was told they were going to take his license away. I'm from San Diego so he asked me if I could help and I said I thought I could. It just so happened I was friendly with the assistant chief of police at the time, so I called him and asked if he could do me a favor. He told me that he could, but that I should tell Herbie if he got one more ticket he'd be in terrible trouble. The very next day, Herbie got another ticket but this time it was because he was driving too slow."

Flam was posthumously enshrined into the International Tennis Association Collegiate Tennis Hall of Fame in 1987, the International Jewish Sports Hall of Fame in 1992, and the UCLA Hall of Fame in 2006.

HELPING TENNIS GROW INTO THE OPEN ERA
Pierre Darmon

When Pierre Darmon made an appointment to meet me for a chat, he suggested we rendezvous in front of the Tenniseum, the Normandy-styled cottage on the grounds of Roland Garros that houses a fabulous museum dedicated to the history of French tennis. It seemed a natural choice of locale and not just because he helped in organizing the Tenniseum or because during the French Open the Tenniseum houses the tournament's Final Eight Club where anyone who reached the singles quarterfinals or doubles semifinals can enjoy tournament hospitality. This Tenniseum venue was actually where Darmon had his office back when he was the tournament director of Roland Garros.

Before we went to enjoy a cup of coffee and talk about his life and times in tennis in the comfort of the Final Eight Club, Darmon wanted to show me something special in the Tenniseum. There, behind a glass wall on display, was a trophy cup. Darmon painted the picture of the importance of the cup with his words, telling how fellow Frenchman Benny Berthet, a jeweler before World War II, fashioned that cup out of tin cans. Berthet, who was born in New York but a Frenchman, became a prisoner of war during World War II and, along with other prisoners, built a tennis court where they were incarcerated. Berthet organized a tournament and designed the trophy, which was rather impressive looking.

"He was Jewish, too, and I was very, very close to him," said Darmon, of his friend, who served as France's Davis Cup captain from 1955 through 1965 and for whom the annual pre-Roland Garros charity day was named for many years. "His story, it's really a fantastic story."

Darmon, a French Open singles finalist and Wimbledon doubles finalist in 1963, was born on January 14, 1934 in Tunis, Tunisia. At age 17, he traveled to live on his own in Paris and France became his home. Initially, he was thinking he would attend the Sorbonne for university and pursue tennis, but doing both was difficult and he chose tennis over studying. Still a Tunisian citizen, his decision to give up his studies led to some consequences — he was obligated to serve in the Tunisian army for two-and-a-half years. "At that time, we were involved in the Algerian War, so when I stopped my studies I had to go to the army. Since I was the No. 1 Tunisian player at that time as such there was a place where sports people had a facility so during the season — the summer — we could play tennis and during the winter we had to go and serve in Algeria."

Being Jewish was just a fact of life for Darmon, who is not particularly religious, and said his religious affiliation had no bearing whatsoever on his career: "I don't think that was any significance at all. I never felt all through my years in tennis that there was any significance to whether I was or was not Jewish." One year he was planning on playing the Maccabiah Games but instead he had to go to Algeria to take part in the war.

For Darmon, playing on the French Davis Cup team was a particular favorite memory. He competed in 34 Davis Cup ties from his first appearance in the international team competition in 1956. He had an impressive 44-17 singles record, but won only three of seven doubles matches. He holds the record for most

Pierre Darmon

wins and most singles victories for a French Davis Cup player and is second - by one tie - behind Francois Jauffret for most Davis Cup ties played.

As impressive as Darmon's tennis career was, it was when he became involved in the business aspect of tennis that he truly had a major impact in the sport. Retired from tennis in 1968, Darmon dedicated himself to seeing tennis through the growing pains of going from an amateur game to an international professional sport.

"I got involved in the French association," Darmon said. "I was picked to run Roland Garros, being like the general manager, which back then was a facility only open during the summer. When I got in there, they only had two contracts — Slazenger balls was on the leaderboard because they gave the balls to play with for free and there were four Coca-Cola signs and that contract was per year and just $1,000. That was what I found.

"It was 1973 when I was also the (French Open) tournament director and I was the one negotiating for bringing sponsors. I was the one who had negotiations to bring BNP Paribas in as a sponsor. But, in fact, I was indirectly dealing with them. The one who really made the deal for BNP was Benny Berthet."

Darmon's position as tournament director at Roland Garros was initially a volunteer position, after five years when he was provided some income for the position, he admitted it was basically a "symbolic" gesture.

One of his favorite accomplishments was borrowing the idea of exclusively located box seats that he saw during a Davis Cup match in Rome. He brought a similar concept to Roland Garros, having prime boxes installed on the stadium court: "I am proud about that because today these boxes are sold for $80,000 Euros, each box. And this is a lot of revenue. And they're in the best position to see a match."

When the ATP started as the men's union in 1973, Darmon was asked to be a founding board member: "I created, with Jack Kramer, the first ATP office in Europe. And you see how life is that Benny Berthet had a big building on the Champs Elysee that he was the owner of and he gave us a little space where we could start a little ATP office in Europe." Eventually Darmon became the Vice President for ATP: Europe, which by then was headquartered in Monte Carlo.

When he moved on from his Roland Garros position with the French Federation of Tennis, Darmon took a position with ProServ, an American management company, as their European Director from 1979 through 1990. He returned to the ATP Europe office as the Chief Executive from 1990 through 1996.

"You cannot compare something so different as the playing and the business and politics," said Darmon, who finally quit playing tennis at age 77 in 2011. "I really must say I enjoyed every moment of my playing and then working and still am enjoying. I cannot complain."

Darmon married Mexican player Rosie Reyes, a Roland Garros doubles champion, more than 50 years ago, and they have three children and four grandchildren. He was inducted into the International Jewish Sports Hall of Fame in 1977. And in November 2002, the ITF honored Darmon with their Davis Cup Award of Excellence.

NEVER A DEMURE ENGLISHWOMAN
Angela Buxton

From the moment Angela Buxton was born on August 16, 1934 in Liverpool, England, she was a child of privilege who would be raised to go after whatever goals she set for herself. It's no wonder that the child of Harry Buxton, a successful entrepreneur who owned a chain of movie theaters, and his wife, Violet, never felt a necessity to conform to the typical life envisioned for women of the time.

As World War II approached, the Buxtons decided that Angela, then 6 years old, along with her mother and brother, would seek safe refuge in South Africa while Harry stayed behind in England to look after his business. The Buxtons, minus Harry, would settle in Capetown, but Angela would attend Yeovil Convent in Johannesburg for four years of her stay. Being a Jewish girl in a convent turned out not to be all that unusual or lonely.

"I have very fond memories of being at the convent," Buxton said. "There were other Jews there, too, and the nuns were very kind to us all. And we were allowed to leave the room when the prayers were being said since we weren't Catholics."

It was as an 8-year-old at Yeovil that Buxton was introduced to tennis — playing was compulsory. Quickly taken with the sport, Angela played every day and her swift progress did not go unnoticed. She was selected as a girl "who stood out," which resulted in a free lesson once a week from the South African national tennis coach. Angela remembers the lessons as if they were given yesterday: "We would go along in twos, a half hour for each two, so it would be 15 minutes each. We thought that was great. Of course, today, it would be laughable. But we all thought it was wonderful and I did play on the school's second team by the time I was 10 or 11, which was pretty impressive since the school went up to 18."

With the war well behind England, Angela and the family returned home. It was 1946, she was 12, and would soon become a child from a broken home. Her mother relocated them to Llandudno, North Wales, where her own parents resided. Angela, who went off to a nearby boarding school, soon discovered that tennis wasn't easy to pursue in Llandudno; for one thing the weather wasn't idyllic for the sport as it was in South Africa. There was no denying that compared with her contemporaries she was a standout — none of them had much opportunity to pursue tennis during the war years, if at all. George Mulligan — a coach from near Liverpool — would come once a week to North Wales and Angela was allowed to take private lessons with him. It didn't take long for Mulligan to see a budding star in his midst.

"He was very handsome and everybody had a crush on him," Angela remembered of Mulligan. "He said to me one evening, 'Do your parents ever come here?' and I said, 'Yes, my mother brings me back on Sunday evening.'" So the next Sunday, Mulligan took the opportunity to speak with Violet, telling her that Angela had above average tal-ent and should be playing in

Angela Buxton

tournaments. Not very well versed on the culture of the ten-nis world, Violet responded with the only tennis knowledge she could drum up, according to Angela, "My mother said to him, 'What do you mean? Wimbledon?'" said Buxton, laugh-ing at the memory. He told her he meant junior tournaments and that if she could find someplace for me to stay in the area between Liverpool and Southport he would train me further and enter me into some junior tournaments."

Mulligan, anticipating the arrival of Angela, raved to his club members about the young natural talent he'd discov-ered, but having been on summer vacation, Buxton remem-bers her introduction at his club was a disaster: "He told all these people he had a girl with potential and then I threw the ball up and missed it completely," she said. "I'd never felt so embarrassed in all my life." Luckily, the setback turned out to be brief and shortly thereafter she was entering — and win-ning — junior events in the area.

Next stop: London. Angela and her mother would eventually move to the city in 1950 when she expressed an interest in pursuing tennis instead of following the usual path for well-to-do young ladies: "They used to finish off girls in Switzerland," Buxton recalled. "You'd learn how to run a big household, how to entertain, keep a husband happy." Although her father knew little about tennis — showing movies was Harry's expertise, not keeping score of tennis matches — he was dedicated to enabling his daughter to follow her dreams.

In London, she would join Queen's Club, a venue which today hosts the famous Wimbledon men's tune-up tournament. The choice of Queen's Club was simple according to Buxton: "It was an exclusive club, but there was no anti-Semitism there at all and at other clubs there was." She also would spend a year studying domestic science at the Polytechnic Institute.

Her first Wimbledon experience came in 1952 as a lucky loser. She fell in the first round, but in the Plate event — a separate tournament that used to be held for the Wimbledon first-round losers — she advanced to the quarterfinals. The experience offered Angela a clear picture of where she stood in the world of tennis and what she learned was that she had vast room for improvement. Angela immediately knew the place to make the necessary repairs to her game would be California. She asked her father to finance an extended trip to the United States to which he readily agreed as long as her mother went along and that she made one promise to him: "He was in the cinema business so it appealed to him very much that I would go to California as long as I would visit the studios and say I was Harry Buxton's daughter."

With the backing from her father secured, Angela went ahead and made all the arrangements by herself. Looking at that now in the context of today's world of tennis she said, "I did all the arrangements myself. I went to the library and found out where all the tournaments were, like in Riverside and Bakersfield, and entered them all from England. I found out the place to play was the LA Tennis Club and a chap called Perry Jones was running it so I wrote to him. I mean, looking back, that's what it takes. You can't expect to be successful if your parents are pushing you. At the time this trip was organized, I was 17."

The Buxtons rented an apartment for six months on the tree-lined block overlooking the LA Tennis Club and settled in. She started to play at the LA Tennis Club, but a few weeks later the arrangements she made fell apart. Jones approached her with the bad news: "He turned around and gave me my money back and said he's sorry but I couldn't play at the club any longer. I asked, 'why not?' I don't think he actually said it but I found out later that it was because I was Jewish. So there I was overlooking the courts I couldn't play on."

Unwilling to allow the trip to California to become a disappointment, Angela went about resolving the problem by "turning a disadvantage into an advantage." Research led to the La Cienega public courts, which was a treasure trove location for tennis. Pancho Gonzalez played there because he also was "excluded" from private clubs. And it was at La Cienega where she took lessons from the great tennis legend, Bill Tilden. She also secured a temporary job working at Arzy's, the racket shack at La Cienega.

In the spring of 1953, back in England, Angela felt she was ready to be a contender. But in April she suffered a humiliating 6-0, 6-0 loss to Doris Hart, the reigning Wimbledon champion, at the Bournemouth Hardcourt Championships. Disheartened, she believed she'd just been wasting her father's money by pursuing tennis and was going to dedicate herself to becoming a dress designer. Nevertheless, she didn't totally abandon tennis and in October 1953, Angela decided to conclude her tennis career in Israel, playing at the Maccabiah Games. As luck would have it, Angela blossomed at the Games, defeating the top 10-rated Anita Kanter from the United States 6-2, 6-3 to win the singles gold medal. She also secured gold in the doubles.

"It was a wonderful experience," said Buxton, of participating in the Maccabiah Games. "I have such fond memories of it. All the footballers came along to cheer me on. I made some wonderful friends that are still friends. In my particular case, that's when I virtually announced to everyone I was Jewish. I thought that would be fun to go with all these other people from different sports and go to Israel to play tennis. This was very big in the international press that I had won two gold medals. People wanted to know what the Maccabiah Games were and they were the Jewish Olympics, so I had announced that I was Jewish."

Instead of the Maccabiah Games being her good-bye to tennis, it acted as her impetus to refocus herself on the sport. During that Bournemouth Hardcourt Championships where she lost to Hart, she had also met Jimmy Jones, a

Daily Mirror sportswriter, the owner of a tennis magazine, and an accomplished teaching pro. He had offered to help her at the time, but she turned him down. On her voyage back to England from Israel, she formulated a plan: She'd now reach out to Jimmy Jones for help. Jones offered a new and different approach to tennis for Angela, stressing that tennis is not just about hitting tennis balls. There were tactical strategies to be learned and a whole psychology to the art of playing winning tennis. Almost immediately, Angela went from being on the fringes of the sport in England to being invited onto the 1954 and 1955 Wightman Cup team for her country. In 1955, she would be a Wimbledon singles quarterfinalist.

Just one year later, Angela Buxton would earn international headlines, and not just because she would have her most successful moment in singles by reaching the Wimbledon final, losing to American Shirley Fry 6-3, 6-1. Angela's fame would be forever tied to the doubles arena and a special and unique winning partnership. In England's world of tennis, despite proving herself of doubles star quality, Angela was not paired with a player of equal talent. Nothing against Pat Hird, but continuing to play doubles with her would hold Angela back. That's what Jones told her, and that's what he suggested she tell the Wightman Cup captain when she called to set things up with Angela in 1956. She followed Jones' advice, which left her without a doubles partner when she arrived at the Bournemouth tournament. In a last-minute, one-off pairing, Angela and Darlene Hard played together and won the title.

But it would be at the French Championships and Wimbledon when two outsiders — Angela Buxton, an upper-class Jewish girl from England, and Althea Gibson, a poor African-American who grew up in New York City — would team together to make magical history, winning both titles. A British national newspaper reported their Wimbledon victory with the headline "Minorities Win." Gibson would also win the French singles title in 1956, and the Wimbledon and U.S. singles trophies in 1957 and 1958.

It was Jones who urged Angela to pursue Gibson as a doubles partner: "No one would even speak to her, let alone play with her," Buxton said. "She was always on her own. My coach said to me, you spend a lot of time with Althea, how about playing with her? I said to him, 'Why don't you ask her if she wants to play with me? Because if she doesn't want to, she'll say no to you but might not to me.' She said yes, she'd like to play with me. We entered the French and we won and we kept it going through Wimbledon."

That would be the beginning of a lifelong friendship between Angela and Althea, a bond that remained until Gibson's death in late September 2003. Gibson not only briefly secured a doubles partner; she became an extended member of the Buxton family.

"My mother was always brought up to help people if you're in a position to help them," Buxton said. "It was a foregone conclusion when someone like Althea came along and had no place to stay, and was with little money, that she would come live with us and she did."

In fact, when Violet Buxton was approached by their London landlord that summer of 1956 with the message that another tenant had complained the family had a black person visiting, she was appalled. Violet suggested the landlord tell the person objecting to come see her themselves. That was the last mention of any issue with Gibson staying in the building.

Later in life, when Gibson was ill and living in poverty in New Jersey, it was Buxton who went about raising money for her good friend, setting up a foundation that would raise $100,000, although much to the dismay of Buxton all the money never made it into Gibson's hands. On one occasion when Buxton was in her South Florida apartment — these days she splits her time between the U.S. and Manchester, England — Gibson called to say she was thinking of ending her life. Buxton was cooking Friday night Sabbath dinner, but quickly turned off the stove and spoke to Gibson for hours, eventually talking her out of doing anything drastic.

For Angela, her time in the upper-echelon of the tennis world turned out to be fleeting. In August 1956 while at a tournament in New Jersey, her right wrist swelled up and she was placed in a cast for six weeks. She would return to tennis, even to win the Maccabiah Games singles title for a second time in 1957, but the wrist became a chronic problem and she soon was forced to retire from the game.

"Today you can get better from tenosynovitis," said Buxton, with a hint of disappointment that the proper treatment wasn't known in her era. "It happens from overuse of the wrist and it's very painful. You can hear a grating noise when you move. Today, a good surgeon can open the wrist, scrape the adhesion, have you do rehab and you're back playing in six months. Those days, they put you in a cast which happens to weaken your wrist. I was 20 when it happened so I only had two or three years when I was at the top of the game."

Although Buxton admits the sudden end of her tennis career came as a shock, she was not one to sit around moaning about her fate. She would work as a fashion designer, a tennis coach and as a tennis journalist in her post-playing life.

Angela's personal life also changed when she married attorney Donald Silk in February 1959 and had three children: Benjamin, Joseph and Rebecca. When the 1967 Six-Day War broke out in Israel, Silk, a prominent Zionist, took the family to Israel for six months. "With three tiny children we volunteered to go to a kibbutz and off we went," she said, remembering she even contemplated moving permanently to Israel. "I was married to the chairman of the Zionist organization of Great Britain and Ireland. We held a rally at Albert Hall, which he ran. Israel needed volunteers to help rebuild and there we were in North Galilee, right under Damascus."

It turned out that Silk was against relocating to Israel, so the family returned to England, where in 1970, the couple separated. That's when she joined forces with her former coach, Jimmy Jones, to start the Angela Buxton Center in Hampstead, located in the northern part of London. They kept the center going until 1988, when it was sold.

Buxton, who was inducted into the Jewish Sports Hall of Fame in 1981, remains a familiar face as well as a force to be reckoned with around the international tennis community. At 79, Angela remains feisty and fair-minded, and is still unable to let go of the fact that despite repeated attempts to join the All-England Lawn Tennis Club, she remains on the outside looking in. Traditionally, Wimbledon singles champions are invited to be members at the All-England and many of the Wimbledon doubles champions who apply are also extended membership. Never one known to be shy, Angela has repeatedly inquired as to why she has been denied membership and insists she's never received a reasonable explanation. She says the club has just told her to be "patient." Not surprisingly, Angela's conclusion is along the lines that the club is primarily anti-Semitic. When asked in 1981 on the British TV program "Nationwide" why she's not an All-England Club member her response was "I'm Jewish; it's as simple as that."

When I inquired as to why Buxton hasn't ever been made a member of the All-England during my annual visit to cover Wimbledon in June 2013, the club's public relations department, headed by the wonderful Johnny Perkins, admitted I was one of a great many reporters to pose that question during the years. Always wanting to be helpful, Perkins delivered the party line — that the All-England Club doesn't address issues of membership, individual members or religion of their members — with a sympathetic smile. That said, I was able to get my hands on a copy of the membership book and while there is no way to know for sure whether anyone is Jewish, there are members who definitely have last names considered to be traditionally Jewish.

Buxton is actually aware that there have been a few Jewish club members; she's just not one of them. The likelihood is that Buxton's outspoken, straight-to-the-point approach to life doesn't fit into the mold of a proper All-England Club member, which certainly hasn't helped her cause. For Angela, it's probably more an issue of being refused membership rather than desperately wanting to be a member that continues to motivate her outrage. After all, she has spent her whole life breaking down unfair barriers and she's not about to stop now.

CHANGING DIRECTION: DOING IT HER WAY
Renee Richards

Unless someone was living under a rock in the late 1970s, they knew who Renee Richards was even if they weren't a tennis fan. After all, it was kind of hard to miss — or ignore — the headlines about the man who became a woman and was suing for the right to play the 1977 U.S. Open as a woman. When Richards won the right to participate, as a woman, in that 1977 U.S. Open, and other women's tournaments, she became the only player in history to play top-level tennis as a man and a woman — although possible, it's highly unlikely that anyone will follow in Richards' footsteps in that regard.

Richards started life as Richard Raskind on August 19, 1934, the youngest child of two physicians — his father was an orthopedic surgeon, his mother a psychiatrist. Richards, who grew up in the leafy New York City quasi-suburban community of Forest Hills, described in her first memoir *Second Serve* how an older sister would push her penis into his body and say 'Now you're a little girl.' If that was not disturbing enough, he also revealed that his mother would, at times, dress him in a little girl's slip instead of traditional boys' clothes.

Despite coming out of that childhood with a feminine image of himself, hardly surprising under the circumstances, Dick was outwardly the total package of the all-American man: tall, good-looking, intelligent and athletic. Publicly, he was living a life that would make other men jealous — attending Yale, where he was the captain of the tennis team, going to medical school at the University of Rochester, serving as a naval lieutenant, becoming a world-class ophthalmologist, marrying a model and having a son. Dick was so popular at Yale that he was asked to join a fraternity that extended few invites to fellow Jewish students.

Throughout that whole period, Dick was unable to totally suppress his urge to be a woman. At college, unbeknownst to others, he would shave his legs. At times, he would dress in women's clothing in private. At one point, after taking female hormone injections off and on, Raskind moved to Paris and lived as a transgender individual. He traveled to Casablanca, Morocco, where there was a doctor who performed sex reassignment surgery that was still unavailable in the United States. In the end, Dick's medical background overtook his urge to finally become Renee, a name which means reborn in French, and was how he had begun to refer to his female persona. He was worried that rumors he heard that the clinic lacked proper hygiene for surgeries were accurate, so he left and went home still a man.

Dick went on with life and was a well-known amateur tennis player in the East. He even played at the U.S. Nationals with his best result being two second-round finishes in 1955 and 1957.

Following the dissolution of his three-year marriage to Barbara and countless times in therapy to deal with his Renee side, in 1975, Richard Raskind underwent sex reassignment surgery to become Renee Richards. His son, Nick, was 3 at the time and until he was 8 was uninformed his father was now a woman — Renee would dress

Renee Richards

as a man, complete with a wig, when she spent time with her son. To this day, even as an adult in his early 40s, Nick Raskind calls Renee "Dad," as that is who Renee is to him.

In talking to National Public Radio's Neal Conan in 1977 to promote her second book *No Way Renee: The Second Half of My Life*, Richards spoke of surgery: "I sought out Dr. Harry Benjamin," said Richards, noting that it was Benjamin, an endocrinologist and sexologist who coined the phrase transsexual, and who treated Christine Jorgensen, the first famous face of transsexualism in the United States. "Harry took care of me and counseled me through those turbulent years and got me started on my hormonal treatment with estrogen. And I was very lucky when he referred me to Dr. Roberto Granato in New York, who was the surgeon who performed the surgery on me. So I, actually, was very fortunate. I wasn't so fortunate in the public's acceptance…"

It was Renee's initial impulse to keep her previous identity as Richard Raskind under wraps. She was so focused on remaining a private citizen that she chose to relocate herself — and her ophthalmologic practice — across the country to Southern California. She just wanted to live life as the woman she always felt she longed to be. Before she left, she received some important counsel from a longtime pal involved in the East Coast tennis scene: "My gynecologist in New York, who is a very close friend of mine, gave me some advice that would come to hit home years later," Richards told Neal Conan during their interview. "He said, 'You're a perfectly normal woman now, except that you look like you've had a hysterectomy. But don't try to play tennis out there when you move to California, because nobody is going to not notice that windup on the forehand that you have.' I didn't really believe Don — it's Don Rubell — and I did play as an amateur in California, trying to remain quiet about it."

As it turned out, Rubell's forewarning was accurate and he came to the opinion with good knowledge. Rubell was well entrenched in the New York tennis community. His father, Phil, was a teaching pro and even reached the finals at the over-90 world tennis championships. His younger brother, the late Steve Rubell, a co-owner of the Studio 54 discotheque, played No. 1 singles for Syracuse University. His wife, Mera, was the U.S. President of Ellesse, the Italian company that dressed many top players in the '70s and '80s. His son, Jason, would be all-American and an ACC singles champion while playing at Duke. And Don himself, was the captain of the Cornell University team when he was there, played at the U.S. Nationals, and ranked third in the East behind Gene Scott and Herb Fitzgibbon and ahead of one, Richard Raskind.

If she had listened to Rubell and stayed away from tennis in California, it's likely life would have gone on under the radar for Renee. But in the end, Renee just couldn't not play — tennis was essential in her life: "Tennis was a refuge because it's something that I love to do, and it was something that I was good at and I could have success at doing. And it was so clear-cut — the geometry of a tennis court and you against your opponent," Renee said on that NPR "Talk of the Nation" radio show. She started to enter local women's tournaments and found herself playing — and winning — the La Jolla championship in 1976. As Rubell predicted, someone, as in a reporter, noticed that windup forehand and the power serve the other women didn't possess. The story broke quickly that a former man was playing at tennis events in California as a woman. Later, in the summer of 1976, Renee's old friend and fellow Yale alum Gene Scott asked whether she wanted to play in the Tennis Week Open at South Orange, New Jersey, a professional women's event where he was the tournament director. She did play, which started a "Keep Renee Richards out of women's tennis" campaign.

Desperate to prevent any possibility of Richards attempting to play the U.S. Open, the United States Tennis Association reacted quickly, saying that Richards would not be welcomed in the U.S. Open women's draw. Now the ball was, so to speak, on Renee's racket — go back to her practice as a prominent eye surgeon, or fight for the right to play tennis as a woman. Never one to let a challenge go by, Renee filed suit against the USTA: "After 30 years of apologizing to myself and to the world in general, I was through apologizing," she wrote in *Second Serve*. "It was time for a savvy lawyer." Renee obviously found the right attorney because in 1977 the New York Supreme Court, after hearing persuasive medical testimony that the surgery and hormonal treatment has indeed turned Renee Richards into a woman, ruled in her favor. She hadn't set out to play at the U.S. Open but now that she was in, she joined the women's circuit. She predicted that because of her age — she already had turned 40 — she could never become a real factor in the women's game. Her best singles ranking was No. 19 and best result was reaching the 1977 U.S. Open doubles final with Betty Ann Stuart (mother of former men's player Taylor Dent), losing to Martina Navratilova and Betty Stove.

Renee traveled the world and despite everyone believing everything regarding her was about her sex switch, it wasn't always the focus. In the Cross-Court Winner chapter on Richards, written by Emily Bazelon in the book *Jewish Jocks: An Unorthodox Hall of Fame*, there was a story that Renee, who had taken to wearing a mezuzah after noticing many players wore crosses on necklaces, told of playing a 1977 tournament in Santiago, Chile: "My opponent said, 'I never saw so many people cheering for you. I said, 'You don't understand — this is a Jewish country club.'"

Not surprisingly, the locker room was somewhat divided on whether Renee belonged on the tour. Billie Jean King and Martina Navratilova believed she should be able to play. Chris Evert and Virginia Wade admitted to not being sure.

And there were some players, who would sometimes sing in a whisper the 1966 Left Banke hit, *Walk Away Renee* when they saw Richards around.

In the end, Renee stayed involved in tennis for five years, first playing, and then coaching, most notably working with Navratilova when she won back-to-back Wimbledon titles (1978=79). She then returned to her life as a physician, choosing to return to New York to do so.

As the years have marched on, Richards has had time to look back and think about everything that's happened in her life. While she strongly believes having the sex change operation was unavoidable, she is now not convinced that choosing to be a public curiosity by playing tennis was the right choice: "I made the fateful decision to go and fight the legal battle to be able to play as a woman and stay in the public eye and become this symbol," Renee told Reuters in February of 2007. "I could have gone back to my office and just carried on with my life and the notoriety would have died down. I would have been able to resume the semblance of a normal life. I could have lived a more private life but I chose not to. I have misgivings about that. I am nostalgic about what would have happened if I had done it the other way."

Richards, who was inducted into the Eastern Tennis Hall of Fame in 2000, spent her last day in the operating room of New York Eye and Ear, which she refers to as "the infirmary," on December 18, 2013. In a posting on her Facebook page, Richards told of her final day as a surgeon, saying, "I was born for two things; to play tennis and operate on eyes. It's what I do, it's who I am and now I don't do either anymore. But that's okay. I did what I was meant to do."

ON THE ANALYSTS' COUCH
Allen Fox

Why did Allen Fox become a tennis player?

That proved to be an easy question for Fox, a former player, heralded coach, author, promotional speaker and PhD psychologist, to answer. He had a Jewish mother who wanted him to play. And Jewish sons often tend to do as mamma says.

"My mother, for whatever reason, liked tennis and she decided I would play tennis," said the fit Fox, who at age 74 was taking his daily run in the California hills as we spoke by phone. "We were living in Tucson at the time. She paid one of the University of Arizona tennis players to show me — he gave me two half-hour lessons — and he showed me how to hit the ball, how to hold a racket. And then she set me up on the backboard and said, 'You will practice for an hour a day,' and that's how I started. It's funny. I must have been a good boy at the time because I would practice for an hour a day even if she wasn't home."

Initially, despite his keeping to the practice schedule his mother planned, tennis didn't really hold his interest.

"Did I like it?" asked Fox, rhetorically, "Not particularly. It was developing a skill and it's always somewhat of a positive to develop a skill because any skill you develop makes you feel good." But then there came an aspect of tennis that did capture his attention. It turns out that Fox possessed a competitive nature.

"After playing for three months, they had a tournament at Tucson — a city championship," Fox remembered. "I hadn't even learned to serve yet, so I was serving underhanded and I gave the guy who won a pretty good match. Of course, in Tucson there was hardly anyone any good in the town so it was a very small tournament — only four of us. I was already in the semifinals just by entering. It kind of gave me incentive that I could win this tournament with a little bit of work. The tournament competition suited me, it became very attractive to me to play tournaments and so I became a fanatic practicer."

By the time Fox was in high school, the family had relocated to California and he attended — and played for — Beverly Hills High School. From there, he only moved down the road a piece to UCLA where he became a NCAA champion, taking the doubles title with Larry Nagler in 1960 and the singles trophy in 1961. UCLA also won the NCAA team championships both of those years.

What impressed Fox the most was when he was named the University of California Athlete of the Year his senior year. In his estimation, earning that honor was "tougher than winning tournaments."

As his undergraduate days were coming to a close — he earned a BA in physics in 1961 — Fox was the fourth-ranked tennis player in the country. He was ready to go out and play world-class tennis. But he didn't leave his studies behind, continuing at UCLA for a graduate degree and eventually a PhD in psychology.

His choice to continue his education opened a door to his close friendship with the late Arthur Ashe, who matriculated at the school in 1963 while Fox was working toward his graduate degree.

At one point, Ashe was quoted as saying in relation to Fox, "In those days, to be Jewish in the top ranks of tennis was to encounter a certain amount of prejudice." Without a doubt, as an African American breaking down barriers, Ashe had an understanding of prejudice.

For Fox, the subject of prejudice – anti-Semitism, in his case — was something that had relevance, and, as a broad issue, it presented a bond with Ashe, whom he played doubles with during his first trip to Wimbledon. All that said, Fox pointed out that he was never subjected to any anti-Semitic moments in his tennis life.

Allen Fox

"There was somewhat of a kindred spirit because both of us (Ashe and myself) felt like the outsiders," Fox said. "As a Jew, I felt like an outsider somewhat. The real fact is, I didn't really experience any anti-Semitism. It was more in my mind than it was actually an occurrence. You're thinking — you go into an old-line tennis club, it's kind of like a Woody Allen in "Annie Hall" and you feel like the Jew comes out. But it really wasn't. I was quite accepted by everybody and there was never really any problem being Jewish."

In fact, Fox mentions Perry Jones of the Los Angeles Tennis Club, the same Perry Jones that Angela Buxton remembered returning her money when she was a teenager when she came from Great Britain to train at his club.

"I got a guest membership to the Los Angeles Tennis Club because I was a good player and at the time it was a supposedly restricted place," Fox recalled. "It isn't anymore. Perry Jones, he was the czar of Southern California tennis. Perry Jones was very powerful and I always had a preconceived notion that he wasn't pro-Jewish, but on the other hand, he never did anything to harm me overtly — he did give me a guest membership to the LA Tennis Club."

A Wimbledon quarterfinalist in 1965, Fox won titles at the Cincinnati tournament in 1961, the U.S. Hard Court tournament in 1962, and the 1966 Canadian Championships.

His most successful moment, however, was in 1966 at the Pacific Southwest tournament when he consecutively defeated all four of the reigning Grand Slam champions en route to taking the title: Manuel Santana, Fred Stolle, Tony Roche and Roy Emerson. He also posted career victories over Arthur Ashe, Jimmy Connors, Stan Smith and John Newcombe.

"I'm not crowing about the Smith win as he was only 18, but I'll take it anyway," said Fox, laughing. "Of all the guys, he was my nightmare guy to play later. It's a good thing I got him young."

Fox played on three Davis Cup teams in 1961, '62, and '66, and won a gold medal at the 1965 Maccabiah Games. While he doesn't liken the Maccabiah Games to his other achievements, as someone who refers to themselves as "I'm not a religious Jew, but I am a Jew," participating in the Jewish Olympics was important.

"There's a very good feeling when you play the Maccabiah Games — a family type of feeling," Fox said. "It was very exciting. I hadn't been to Israel before. It was a chance to meet all these Jewish athletes from all over the world. It wasn't the strongest tournament I ever won. It was more an experience than sort of a notch on your tournament belt."

When Fox was finished playing, he started a career as an investment banker where he said he made some money, but not really enough to call it a living. Nevertheless, he felt a pull to keep his relationship going with tennis and turned to college coaching at Pepperdine University. He led Pepperdine men's teams to two NCAA Championship finals and six quarterfinal berths, and to a top-five ranking for 10 consecutive years.

"I felt a freedom to do what I wanted," he said. "Pepperdine was at first like a pastime for me — I didn't consider it a job. It was sort of a fun thing because I wanted to see what it was like to do some coaching. It kind of hooked me in."

His favorite part of coaching was the lasting relationships he made with many of his players. But he admits his radar instinct for which players might succeed on the pro tour could be considered faulty. Brad Gilbert would be one of those players he coached and didn't predict to have the bright career he carved out in the game.

"This is an indication of my coaching talent: I never thought Brad would make a living as a professional tennis player," said Fox, laughing. "I couldn't see how he could do it. It's really very, very hard to tell. He was a transitional player. Gilbert didn't do it the way everybody else did. He didn't hit the ball hard. He had no second serve and couldn't volley, so I couldn't see how he could possibly beat these guys. There's a judgment factor that you can't see from the outside which he had; it's internal — what shot to hit, when, how hard, how close to the lines — he has perfect judgment. You can have every stroke worse than your opponent and still beat them if your judgment is better than theirs."

THE FLYING DUTCHMAN
Tom Okker

In 1968, Arthur Ashe and Tom Okker — two players still considered to be amateurs — played in the final of the first-ever U.S. Open that would include professional players and offer prize money. Ashe would win, defeating Okker 14-12, 5-7, 6-3, 3-6, 6-3, and collected $15 a day for his achievement. Okker, who had status as a "registered player" — meaning he was an amateur who could collect prize money at certain tournaments — scored the $14,000 top prize check for coming in as the runner-up.

Ashe was the first African American man to win a major title. In a country that only recently went through a desegregation process, Ashe's victory stood out to sports and non-sports fans alike.

That final at Forest Hills, however, is not my most vivid memory of Okker. Very early in my career — as in the first few months — I worked for the late Gene Scott, a former U.S. National semifinalist, who went on to have a multifaceted career in the game, highlighted by being a tournament director and publisher of the now defunct *Tennis Week* magazine.

Gene also was an attorney. It would be hard to find many kids from the New York tri-state area who didn't receive a start in the tennis business from Gene. As the newly named editor of *Tennis Week*, one of my perks was that Gene sent me down for the weekend to the Philadelphia tournament, where Okker would team with Wojtek Fibak of Poland to beat Peter Fleming and John McEnroe in a three-set final for the title on Sunday.

I planned on returning to New York after the tournament in the same way I arrived — on the Amtrak train. It provides convenient and pain-free travel between cities on the Eastern Seaboard. When I showed up in the lobby with my suitcase for a ride to the train station — most tournaments are very courteous in providing transportation — Tom Okker also was at the transport desk. When he heard me say I was going to the 30th Street station to get the train back to New York he piped in. He also was heading to New York but was flying. I'm sure I must have frowned as no one from New York would fly to Philly or vice versa. But Okker was moving on from New York so flying made sense. That was when he suggested that instead of taking the train, I should fly with him, as why shouldn't we have each other's company on the trip? I guess it sounded kind of decadent to fly between the two places, so I agreed. Plus, LaGuardia was actually an easy place for my mother to come pick me up.

It sounded like a great idea until the moment they were boarding the plane. This was no jet — it was a small propeller number that only had about three steps up to get into and probably had about 12-16 passenger seats. I remember I wasn't so happy as the plane looked like it arrived straight from World War II service and I must have envisioned the pilot telling everyone it was time to start flapping their arms to keep the plane aloft and not to stop until we landed.

Tom Okker

Tom obviously saw my concern. It was at that point he reached to his neck and pulled out a necklace crammed with hanging charms. As he told me that we'd be fine because he had all his good luck medals on, I noticed that two stood out: one was a Jewish symbol and the other representing Christianity. I asked him about it and he explained his father was Jewish and his mother wasn't and he thought it was advisable to take his luck from all possible sources. He filled in the religious conversation by saying he saw himself as Jewish and had even played at the Maccabiah Games in Israel, winning the singles and mixed doubles titles in 1965.

We arrived in New York safely — it must have been Tom's good luck trinkets — and that remains the only time I've ever flown that route.

Thomas Samuel Okker was born on February 22, 1944 in the Netherlands, a country that was under the occupation of Nazi Germany. The Netherlands had hoped to stay neutral when war broke out in 1939, but in mid-May 1940, the Germans bombed Rotterdam and the next day the country surrendered. The Dutch royal family took refuge in Britain, but the rest of the Dutch stayed behind to deal with being an occupied country. Prior to 1940, there were 140,000 Jews in Holland, but by the time the Netherlands were liberated in May 1945 only 30,000 had survived.

Growing up in a post-war-torn country, it took awhile for life to get back to normal and live beyond the basics. For Okker, it wasn't until he turned 10 that he was introduced to tennis. When he started winning junior tournaments, Tom thought that pursuing tennis seriously would be fun.

Finding a path to the international tennis circuit, Okker would end up winning 31 singles titles and reaching the final of 24 additional events. He would rank among the top 10 for a number of years with a career high of No. 3 in March 1974. His best Grand Slam result was reaching that 1968 U.S. Open final, but he also reached the semifinals at the other three majors during his career. In 2014, he still sits high on the list of Top 50 all-time Open Era title leaders at No. 24 in the world with his 31 singles trophies.

Okker also was a prominent doubles player and on February 5, 1979, he became the fourth doubles player in the history of the official ATP doubles rankings to become ranked No. 1 — he would occupy the top spot for a total of 11 weeks in his career. He won two Grand Slam doubles titles: at the 1973 French Open with John Newcombe and at the 1976 U.S. Open with Marty Riessen. In all, Okker won 78 doubles titles, which was a record until Australian Todd Woodbridge broke it in 2005.

Okker, who was one of the first to frequently use a heavy topspin shot, competed in 13 Davis Cup ties between 1964 and 1981, amassing a 15-20 win-loss record.

When Okker decided it was time to put down his racket in 1981, he became an art broker, first as a founding partner of Jaski Art Gallery in Amsterdam and, in 2005, opened Tom Okker Art in Hazerswoude-Dorp, the town outside of Amsterdam where he lives. Okker's gallery is all things related to the CoBrA movement of art, which highlights abstract expressionist artists from Copenhagen, Brussels and Amsterdam.

Okker was enshrined into the International Jewish Sports Hall of Fame in 2003.

PIONEERING FOR WOMEN'S TENNIS
Julie Heldman

Born into a true American tennis family, it would have been impossible for Julie Heldman to escape turning to tennis in her life.

Heldman's father, Julius, was the national junior champion in 1936 and her mother, Gladys, was the Texas state champion in the 1950s. So ingrained in tennis, it comes as no surprise that when the Heldmans were looking for the right summer camp to send their daughter their choice leaned toward the sport and the Hoxie Tennis Camp in Greater Detroit. She would attend for the first time as an 8-year-old and would continue to spend summers there for years to come. By the time she was 12, Julie won the Canadian 18-and-under title — it was the beginning of her existence as an exceptional tennis player.

A star student at private schools in New York City, Julie graduated high school at just 16. That fall she enrolled at Stanford University, and during the summer between her freshman and sophomore years she won the national junior

18-and-under title, matching her father's achievement from 1936.

In 1965, Julie spent her spring semester studying abroad in France. When the semester was over, she stayed in Europe to try her luck playing the European circuit. Luck was indeed in her corner — she became a semifinalist at the Italian Championships and made it to the round of 16 at Wimbledon. Collegiately,

Julie Heldman

she reached the singles and doubles finals of the 1964 National Collegiate tennis events. Graduating in December 1966 with a degree in history, Heldman felt she had enough of the real world for awhile and decided to drop out — literally. She moved to a hippie commune in California. A few months later, however, Heldman decided to drop back into real life and headed home to New York, and then eventually returned to California to a teaching job at the Berkeley Tennis Club.

By 1968, Heldman was back to playing against the best players in the world. She took part in the 1968 tennis test event at the Olympics held in Mexico. In 1969, Julie was part of the U.S. Maccabiah Games team, scoring the ultimate hat trick: winning the singles, doubles and mixed doubles trophies. An elbow injury would sideline Julie in the summer of 1970, but that would not keep her from taking part in the true birth of the professional women's tour on September 23, 1970, in Houston, Texas.

What Julie is most known for is being one of the "Original 9"— Billie Jean King, Rosie Casals, Judy Tegart Dalton, Kerry Melville Reid, Nancy Richey, Peaches Bartkowicz, Kristy Pigeon, Val Ziegenfuss and, of course, Heldman. In 1970, these women would buck the system by challenging the ruling arm of American tennis — the United States Lawn Tennis Association. Aware that the prize money at USLTA events was unfairly skewed in favor of the men, these nine women set out to find a more lucrative solution.

It was Julie's mother, Gladys, the publisher/owner of the *World Tennis* magazine, who is considered the founder of the professional women's tour. Gladys was friendly with Joseph Cullman III, the Chairman of the Board of Phillip Morris — a successful American Jewish businessman who liked tennis. Cullman would agree to sponsor a Virginia Slims circuit — "You've Come a Long Way Baby" was the slogan for the cigarette branded as Virginia Slims and for the new women's tennis circuit. The Original 9, including Julie, played in the first Virginia Slims event in Houston despite threats by the USLTA to ban them from their tour. Pretty soon, many of the women were choosing the Virginia Slims tour as the place to showcase their tennis.

A natural baseliner who rarely ventured to the net, Heldman's game was predicated on tactical decisions and accurate ball placement. In 1974, Julie reached the U.S. Open semifinals, falling to eventual champion Billie Jean King.

When Heldman's playing days came to an end as a result of a shoulder injury in 1975, she would spend time in the media world writing for her mother's magazine, as well as serving as a radio and television commentator. In 1976, she made history by becoming the first woman to talk the talk on a televised men's match at the Challenge Cup in Hawaii.

Eventually, she would move away from tennis to attend UCLA Law School and would pursue a legal career through the early 1980s. In 1985, she decided to work with her husband, Bernard Weiss, in the eyeglass frame business, which she did until retiring in 2000.

In April 2012, Julie would join the other members of the Original 9 for a reunion organized in the finest of styles by The Family Circle Cup tournament and the WTA in Charleston, South Carolina. Heldman would write a blog about the reunion for the official WTA Tour website and had these comments to make about the get-together nearly 42 years after the nine delivered women's tennis into the modern era.

"We were all looking forward to Charleston, but no one was prepared for just how magical the reunion would be. It wasn't just the honors, though frankly they were pretty wonderful. And it wasn't just the gratitude of former and current champions for what we had done. … Saturday night, our last in Charleston, we stayed up past midnight signing mementos for each other and for the WTA, and none of us wanted to leave, so that we could squeeze out another few minutes with each other. We've all vowed to stay in touch, and we're already talking about the next reunion, when we can once again laugh and talk and treasure old times. Rosie (Casals) says we shouldn't wait another 40 years because it'll be too late. We're strong-minded women. We won't wait."

A MESSIANIC JEW IN OUR MIDST
Brian Gottfried

When tennis fans think to the protégés of famed tennis coach Nick Bollettieri, most reel off the names Jimmy
Arias, Aaron Krickstein, Andre Agassi, Anna Kournikova
and Maria Sharapova. What most people don't know is that
Brian Gottfried, a serve-and-volleyer, former world No. 3
and 1977 French Open finalist was Bollettieri's first pro success story.

Say what, you say?

Yes, Brian Edward Gottfried, born in Baltimore,
Maryland, on January 27, 1952, was the first of the many top
10-ranked players to work under Bollettieri's tutelage. The
Gottfried family moved to South Florida when Brian was
young and he was 9 years old when Nick discovered him in a
North Miami park, only one year after Brian first discovered
tennis.

Brian's dad was involved in a number of service organiza-
tions and one day Eddie Herr, a guru of junior tennis events
in South Florida, addressed one of the groups asking for volunteers to house some juniors who would be in town to play

for the Sunshine Cup and Orange Bowl. The Gottfrieds, who knew nothing about tennis, agreed to house some Japanese players and it was the beginning of their love affair with the game: "The Japanese players offered me a racket and I went out to watch them play and that's what got me," Gottfried said. "I had never played tennis. I was an athlete and played baseball, and my dad was an athlete, so sports was always a part of our lives."

Fairly quickly after picking up a racket, Brian was hooked and his interest only grew after he won a junior doubles tournament soon thereafter. He enjoyed being at the park and playing — it was fun. When Bollettieri saw him play, he immediately asked the Gottfrieds whether their son could spend summers with him pursuing tennis. Bollettieri spent the winters in Puerto Rico, but took different jobs during the summer back in the U.S.

"The first summer job that he had that I went with him was in Springfield, Ohio — the Springfield Country Club, so I went to live with him in Springfield for three months," Gottfried said. "I'd kind of be his ball machine. I would be hitting balls to players he was teaching and he would be standing beside them giving them a lesson."

It was on that first trip with Nick that Brian encountered his only tennis-related anti-Semitic incident but at the time he didn't understand what was really going on: "I was 9 years old and at the Springfield Country Club and every evening Nick would send me out for dinner and I didn't know why," Brian told me. "I didn't think about it and I would go out to this diner down the street and I would sit down and they used to give me extra applesauce. I could tell something was up and I wondered about it but didn't know. I later found out that they didn't let Jews in the restaurant at the country club. It was a different time, so I could just walk down the street on my own. So it was no big deal."

By the time Brian was 12, he won his first national title and would end up winning 14 national junior trophies, which led to him being considered one of the top five junior players in the United States. When he was 15, Brian went off to the Baylor School, a military academy in Chattanooga, Tennessee,

Brian Gottfried

where the tennis coach was Chris Evert's uncle, Jerry. Roscoe Tanner, the future Australian Open champion and Wimbledon finalist, was one of his classmates. The structure of a military academy, coupled with the freedom of being away from home, was a difficult combination for Brian, who discovered the power of partying and girls while at Baylor. He would end up being sent home from the boarding school, although he eventually was allowed to come back to take tests and earn a diploma.

From there, Brian went off to Trinity University in San Antonio, Texas, where he would room with future U.S. Davis Cupper Dick Stockton. He would spend three years at Trinity, helping the school win the NCAA team championship title in 1972.

"There was no question at all that back when I was coming up you had to play college tennis," Gottfried remembered. "You couldn't go any further. First of all, I started college in 1969 and Open tennis started in 1968 so clearly you really didn't have a goal of playing pro tennis. The best you could do in tennis was to play Davis Cup — that would be the pinnacle of tennis success. You couldn't even dream about becoming a pro — a contract pro – because only a handful of guys did that and they were the gods." During his time at Trinity, Brian realized he was among the best at the collegiate level, which led him to the idea that he could be one of those lucky players to make it as a world-class pro. Forgoing an opportunity to finish college, he left school in 1972 without a degree and headed for the pro circuit.

By 1973, Gottfried proved he was on target for a successful pro career, winning titles at the WCT Johannesburg and Alan King Tennis Classic in Las Vegas. It was no wonder that *Tennis* magazine name Brian its 1973 Rookie of the Year. In all, he would win 25 singles and 54 doubles titles during his career. One of his favorite tournaments was Vienna. He won there on four occasions and, in 1983, it would become the final singles title of his pro career. "Vienna was a favorite for the obvious reason that I won it multiple times," Brian said. "I liked the wiener schnitzel and the bread there, too. We (Brian and his wife, Windy) got to the point we really, really enjoyed Europe. It became very much like a second home even though there were all these different languages."

Like his good friend Harold Solomon, Brian points to being a non-playing member of the 1972 Davis Cup team that journeyed to Romania for the finals as one of the true highlight experiences: "I always talk about that Davis Cup year in 1972," Brian told me. "Eddie Dibbs and I were there as the practice partners. We played in Romania in the final right after the Jewish athletes were massacred at the Olympics. The security and everything that went on around it, playing Romania, it was our country against a Communist country, and then Stan (Smith) and Nasty (Ilie Nastase) were co-ranked No. 1 before that match — there was just a lot of political atmosphere around it. So it was a tennis match played under incredible pressure and for Stan to play like he did, and then our winning. It's just always something I come back to and remember." Taking part in Davis Cup from 1972 through 1982, Gottfried was on the 1978 squad with John McEnroe, Stan Smith and Bob Lutz that beat Great Britain 4-1 in the final held at Palm Springs, California — it was the first U.S. Davis Cup victory since the Americans defeated Romania at Bucharest in 1972.

Although most would point to Brian's reaching the 1977 French Open final as his most prominent achievement in tennis, he has little memory of the 6-0, 6-3, 6-0 drubbing he experienced at the hands of Guillermo Vilas, the Argentine Bull of the Pampas. "I don't think a lot about the French Open because I wasn't on court long enough," said Brian, laughing. "As I tell people when they ask about it, I say, 'Were you at that match? Because I owe you a refund if you were.' It was his day and it wasn't mine. It was wet and cold and I was approaching, and he was sort of laughing at me as I was trying to come in on a day like that. I look at it and I sort of have sympathy with (Roger) Federer when I see him playing (Rafael) Nadal on clay. You can either stay back and have a nice 15-20 ball rally and lose it or you can have a 3- or 4-ball point and get passed — pick your poison! I didn't serve big enough to blow Guillermo off the court and just trying to work the point and come in wasn't getting it done." Despite the French Open loss, the year 1977 treated Brian well — he won a season-high five titles and reached a career-high ranking of No. 3.

During his touring days, Brian lived at the St. Andrews Country Club in Boca Raton, Florida, and was their touring pro. In a bit of coincidence among former Jewish pros, Aaron Krickstein is now the longtime Director of Tennis at the same St. Andrews Country Club. Following his retirement, Brian worked with many players as a coach — Luke Jensen and MaliVai Washington were two of his most well-known pupils.

Eventually, when the ATP Tour opened its headquarters in Ponte Vedra Beach, Florida, Brian moved to northern Florida and assumed a number of roles with the men's tour: Director of Tennis (1989-1995), General Manager (1995-1999), Touring Professional (1999-2006). Since that time, he has thrived as a consultant coach with the Harold Solomon Tennis Institute (2007-2008), Nick Bollettieri Tennis Academy (2009-2010) and now operates the tennis program at the private Bolles School in Jacksonville, Fla., where Brian's adult son, Kevin, once was a student.

What isn't well known about Brian is that within the last 20 years, he has found a different belief when it comes to religion from how he grew up: "I was Bar Mitzvah'ed but after that my parents left me to find my own way," he said. "Tennis became my life. If I wasn't playing on Sunday, it meant everybody stay away from me because I wasn't in the finals and I was upset."

For many years, Brian, who married outside of the faith, followed no particular religious path, nor did his family. But then when his kids were in their teens — his wife started to return to church and their children — son Kevin and daughter Kelly — followed. Brian started to go along to church seeing it as a family outing, but eventually he heard what he was listening to and found he also could believe.

Having remained a good friend with the Gottfrieds after Brian retired from the tour, I was well aware of Brian's choice to follow Jesus, so I just chuckled when I called him the first time to talk for the book to discover he was in the car, "Sure," he said, 'It's a good time to talk now. Why not talk to a Jewish person on his way to church?"

Apparently, since I first mentioned the book to Brian, he'd been giving thought to how he would explain his religious beliefs today: "You've been talking about doing the book and I've been thinking about that, wondering what will I say to Sandy," he admitted. "I'm still not totally sure what to say other than I still very much consider myself Jewish because I think you're born a Jew, my bloodline is Jewish, but I also believe that Jesus is the Messiah so that goes against what a Jew is supposed to think. The very first disciples of Jesus were all Jewish, whether it was Paul or Matthew — all the people he was talking to were Jewish. In my way of thinking, it completes a Jewish thinking in that it should take you a step further — it's a more complete, more encompassing understanding of the law — of the Torah — of the commandments. I call myself a Messianic Jew."

On the Messianic Jewish Alliance of America website, the explanation for Messianic Judaism is that it is "a biblically based movement of people who, as committed Jews, believe in Yeshua (Jesus) as the Jewish Messiah of Israel of whom the Jewish law and Prophets spoke. To many this seems a glaring contradiction. Christians are Christians. Jews are decidedly not Christian. So goes the understanding that has prevailed through nearly two thousand years of history. Messianic Jews call this a mistaken — and even anti-Scriptural — understanding. Historical and Biblical evidence demonstrates that following Yeshua was initially an entirely Jewish concept. Decades upon decades of persecution, division, and confused theology all contributed to the dichotomy between Jews and believers in Yeshua that many take for granted today."

While Brian never played in Israel when the country had a tournament, he had an opportunity to visit the Holy Land with Stan Smith when the two were invited to Vienna to celebrate that tournament's 25th anniversary a number of years ago. From there, the Gottfrieds and Smiths went on to Israel: "That was the most phenomenal trip we've ever been on," Brian said. "We had a great time and did things for the Jewish Federation — clinics and such. Some people from the Federation took us on a tour but it never came up that I had a belief in Jesus as a Jew."

Through his local church in Neptune, Florida, Brian has dedicated himself to doing a prison ministry, which has become a treasured activity of his for many years. One Bible message he keeps close to heart as he lives life with all its twists and turns is that "God promises that, 'I know the plans I have for you, plans that prosper you and not harm you and give you hope for the future.'"

Gottfried was inducted into the Jewish Sports Hall of Fame in 1999. He also has been enshrined into the USTA Florida Hall of Fame (1985), the Intercollegiate Tennis Association Hall of Fame (1990), Trinity University Hall of Fame (2009) and the Florida Sports Hall of Fame (2013).

BEYOND THE BAGEL AND THE MOON
Harold Solomon

Harold Solomon knows exactly what people remember him for and he's more than content with the direction of his fame. He'll always be one-half of the Bagel Twins of tennis with good friend Eddie Dibbs. And he'll always be the guy they named the moon ball for — no one else had the ability of repetitively returning shots with loopy high balls close to the baseline down to such a science.

Harold laughs to this day — about 40 years later — when he thinks about the Bagel Twins moniker: "Everybody remembers the Bagel Twins thing and everybody thinks Eddie is Jewish," Solomon said. "I tell everybody that Eddie (who is actually of Lebanese descent) is a convenient Jew: when it was convenient to be Jewish, he was Jewish; when it was not convenient to be Jewish, he was not Jewish. He always said to me, 'Don't tell anyone I'm not Jewish.' Anything that could help market you — set you apart — was a good thing. We were the Bagel Twins and we tried to get a deal with Lender's Bagels, but it didn't work."

In actuality, what fans should remember Harold Solomon for is his intelligent businesslike approach to tennis. One perfect example of Solomon's acumen was his penchant for moon balling. Harold's bottom line was to be a world-class level tennis player and fulfilling that dream required making smart decisions. He read and heard all the snickers and criticism regarding his moon ball — fellow player Dick Stockton was known to have yelled at him to "hit the ball like a man." Famed British tennis writer Rex Bellamy suggested Solomon's "game was a threat to low flying birds." But Harold didn't care — he was on a course for success.

"I know mine wasn't the preferred way of playing, but it was the only way I was going to play that was going to be effective," Solomon said. "It actually wasn't the way I played all the time, but it (the moon ball) was a shot I used. It was back in the day when everyone had a one-handed backhand and it was really effective to get the ball up high. And it fit in with the image I had of a guy who could go out there and play all day long. Anything that would fit that image, I would promote. If someone said it was going to be in the 90s this week, I'd say, 'I hope it's going to be in the 100s.' When I first started out, I'd play all my matches with track pants on even though it was 95 degrees just to show those guys that I can stay out there all day long. A lot of the guys were defeated before they walked on the court. They used to say, 'Bring your lunch to play against Harold' and that was great."

The fact that Solomon approached tennis with the mind-set of an executive isn't so surprising as his family was deeply entrenched in corporate enterprises — the family business was owning Budget Rent-A-Car franchises.

Harold was born on September 17, 1952 in Washington D.C., the first to arrive of four siblings — sister Barbara was three years younger, brother Mark six years younger, and baby sister Shelley 11 years younger. One day when Harold was 5, he saw his dad, Leonard, playing tennis when they were on vacation in Florida and decided he wanted to play too.

"I asked if I could try and after that it never stopped," he said. "As soon as I picked up the racket I could actually hit the ball. I had pretty good eye-hand coordination. He was pitching me balls and I could hit them over the net right off the bat."

By the time Harold was 8, he won his first tournament.

Harold Solomon

After that, it didn't take long for the Solomon clan to become defined by tennis. To facilitate their playing, the family kept to a unique lifestyle:

"We used to come down to Florida in the winters all the time," Solomon said. "My parents didn't move down here permanently until I went away to college so I was really raised in Maryland. But we were down here in the wintertime from the time I was about 14 until I was 17. We would spend from September to December in Maryland, December to April down here, and April through June we'd be back in school in Maryland. It was really weird. We went to different schools every year because when we were down here we just rented houses."

His time in South Florida helped to solidify lifelong friendships with Dibbs, his Bagel Twin, who he played with the day before our interview in July, 2013, and Brian Gottfried, another Jewish player who was born in Baltimore, Maryland, but moved to Fort Lauderdale in his early youth. And while Solly had his no-nonsense serious side, he didn't miss out doing what most teenage boys like to do.

"The three of us were a good team, we were kindred spirits. Brian and I, we used to always — we were the two goofiest guys — we spent our Christmas vacation cruising up and down Fort Lauderdale beach trying to pick up girls, which we never did," remembered Solly, laughing at the memory. "But I remember we would think we were going to pick them up. I remember driving up and down— and walking up and down — night after night, doing that sort of thing and trying to get lucky. I think the girls got lucky because they didn't hook up with us."

Attending Rice University in Houston, Texas, Harold decided it was time to turn pro at the end of his sophomore year. Later that same year, he was already considered a top player on the tour. It was a special time in the game and he feels privileged to have been a part of it all.

"Tennis was such the cool sport when I was getting into it," he said. "It was the beginning of Open tennis. I think I came up through the most exciting time ever in tennis. All the old guys were still there and you got to play against (Rod) Laver, (Ken) Rosewall, (Roy) Emerson, and then (John) Newcombe, Arthur (Ashe) and that generation — Stan

(Smith), (Ilie) Nastase, and then our group of guys. Then you had (John) McEnroe come in and (Ivan) Lendl come in, and even (Stefan) Edberg and (Andre) Agassi — I even played against Agassi. So it was an amazing group of the best players that ever played and I got to play at the same time."

Always disciplined about his tennis, as was Gottfried, the two would do anything to get the most out of their careers. When, in 1978, Solly made a goal to reach the top 5 in the world, he never missed playing a day for a two-year period, training until he achieved the desired ranking. Both Solomon and Gottfried had a reputation of being obsessive about their dedication to being the best they could be.

"I just hated to lose," Solomon said. "I wanted to make something of myself and I was willing to do whatever it took. They used to kid Brian and I because we used to be signed up all over the practice sheets so they used to just erase us from some of the times we signed up for. Like when we were in Europe at indoor events, we'd get up at 3 a.m. and go practice at 4 in the morning. It didn't matter to us, we'd do whatever we needed to."

One of his most cherished moments in the game was reaching the 1976 French Open final, losing to Italy's Adriano Panatta in four sets: "I always thought I'd win there or get to the final again," Solly admitted. While the French Open victory never happened, 22 career singles titles did.

Another special achievement was being a part of the 1972 and '78 winning U.S. Davis Cup efforts. The '72 win really stands out even though after competing in the first three rounds captain Dennis Ralston didn't play him in the finals against Romania. That was Solomon's first year playing as a pro and he was thrilled to be a part of delivering an internationally renowned title to his country. There was also the fact that the final featured concerns beyond just trying to beat Romania for the title.

"The only time I was ever uncomfortable traveling was the time we went to play the Davis Cup final in Romania the same year as the Olympic massacre in Munich," revealed Solomon, who, along with Gottfried, made for a strong Jewish presence on the U.S. squad. "They were really concerned about us. They took about 1,000 Arabs out of the city of Bucharest; the government just took them out for the week while we were there. We had armed guards the whole time we were there, our own floor in the hotel, guys with machine guns around the court the whole time. That was kind of like a freakish situation."

There was obviously no secret that a guy named Harold Solomon probably could claim Jewish status. Indeed, Harold's parents were Conservative Jews and he was Bar Mitzvah-ed at a Conservative temple. Despite the background, he has strayed away from that more conventional approach to Judaism.

"I've been very much a non-religious person for a very long period of time," he said. "I definitely accept my heritage and where I came from but I would say you would call me a secular Jew. Institutional religion is really not for me." That said, and while Solomon and his wife, Jan, raised their daughter, Rachel, and son, Jesse, with a little bit of temple and a little bit of church, he believes if you asked his kids they would probably say they were Jewish, although he's not really sure why.

Solomon doesn't shy away from telling that during his tennis years he did run up against a couple of anti-Semitic incidents.

In his junior days, Solomon once played a match at Flamingo Park in Miami against a player whose father was the tennis parent from hell. During the match, the father had a few choice anti-Semitic remarks he hurled Solomon's way from the stands. But what he did afterward was even more disturbing: "He wrote letters to like 100 colleges across the United States — it was the most profane letter in the history of the world — I have a copy of the letter at home. He was trying to keep me from getting into school. It was unbelievable."

Another time, when Solomon was playing Rosewall in the River Oaks semifinals, they were embroiled in a long match and Solomon fell to the court at 5-all in the third with cramps: "Some guy in the stands yelled out, "Die, Jew bastard, die."

Except for those occasions, however, Solomon remembers good times and a pleasant environment within the game. He strongly believes that "sports is a great thing to bring people together. I think once people become familiar with each other that familiarity breeds respect."

Always outspoken, by 1978 Solomon found himself as more than just a player — he began to take a role in the politics of the game. Although he was represented at the time by Dell, Craighill, Fentress & Benton, who were the forces behind the ProServ representation agency, it didn't stop him from standing up at an ATP meeting to bring up the fact that the company was involved in too many conflicting aspects of the game. That same day, Donald Dell was on a plane to admonish Solomon for his outburst, which led to the company no longer representing him. He took a place on the player board, eventually was the President of the ATP for a few years in the 1980s, and, even after he stopped playing, went back on the ATP board as well as the WTA board for a time. Nowadays, he leaves the politics to the younger voices in the game.

Initially, when Solomon left the tour in 1990 he went to work in the family business for five years. When the decision was taken to sell their Budget Rent-A-Car operation, Harold returned to his tennis roots. He first coached Mary Joe Fernandez and also worked with Jim Courier, Justin Gimelstob, Monica Seles, Daniela Hantuchova, Anna Kournikova and, more recently, Elena Dementieva and Shahar Pe'er. When Jennifer Capriati came back to the game for her second career — and was ranked in the mid-100s — Solomon delivered her back to a top 10 ranking.

Eventually, however, the travel became tiring so Harold decided to stay closer to home. He opened a boutique academy — The Harold Solomon Tennis Institute in Fort Lauderdale. The focus is on individual attention with the maximum of 20 to 25 kids taking part at any one time. There are never more than two kids on a court, and, at 61 years old, Solomon still spends six or seven hours a day on the court working with his students.

One thing Solomon sees in today's game is that the sport has really changed in the United States, but not so much elsewhere in the world. He believes the difference between today's approach to the sport as compared with the past explains why we're not seeing the American superstars that used to be a given.

"So many Americans are so out of touch about what it takes to be successful these days," he said. "The work ethic is just not the same as it used to be. They have no idea about the concept about building a career — the ingredients that go into it — physically, mentally, technically. They don't grasp the setting goals and going out there and working to realize your goals."

Solomon was enshrined into the Jewish Sports Hall of Fame in 2004.

THE AUSTRALIAN OPEN CHAMPION
WHO ALMOST WASN'T

Brian Teacher

Brian Teacher came from a time when players thought that winning a college tennis scholarship was the ultimate success story and very few could even imagine playing on the international tennis circuit.

His love of tennis came from his mom, who played recreational tennis at Morley Field, a public park in San Diego where the great Maureen Connolly learned to play the game. Brian was born in 1954 and he describes his hometown of San Diego aptly: "In the '50s, it was pretty much a sleepy naval town." Before he was old enough to go to school, Brian would accompany his mother to Morley Field a few times a week when she would play tennis and he would play nearby to the courts.

"I would run around there and watch my mom play," Brian remembered. "I kind of wanted to try and play tennis at an early age so they gave me a racket. I seemed to take a natural liking to it and she would always feed me balls."

As Teacher's interest in tennis grew, his parents started giving him occasional lessons. And then when he was between 10 and 12 years old, he would take weekend clinics at the public facility with Fred Kinney, an editor at the *San Diego Union-Tribune* and avid tennis player.

"There was not that many places to play in San Diego there weren't many clubs," he said. "There was the La Jolla Beach and Tennis Club but that was in La Jolla and I lived more in the center of San Diego. And at the same time you had to have a lot of money to belong to a club and we didn't have enough money."

By the time that Teacher reached his teens, he was even more taken in by tennis. He wanted to do whatever he could to become the best player possible. In his mind he hit the jackpot when he was offered a tennis scholarship to UCLA — it was known as a highly prominent tennis school as well as an academically acclaimed college.

"I was excited to go up there because it was one of the top teams in the country," Teacher said. "They had (Jeff) Borowiak and (Jimmy) Connors there, although when Jimmy won the NCAAs he left to turn pro. I went to UCLA in '72 and pro tennis just came in in '68 so there wasn't a lot of money in it."

While Brian was thrilled to be at UCLA to pick the brain of tennis coach Glenn Bassett, he also expanded his tennis horizons by hopping in the car and going to Rolling Hills. That's where he would take occasional lessons from Robert Landsdorp, a Dutchman born in Indonesia who had a guiding hand in molding many of the greats including Tracy Austin, Lindsay Davenport, and Maria Sharapova.

When Teacher entered UCLA he had no intention of pursuing a pro career, it just wasn't the given natural progression for most back then although former Bruins Arthur Ashe and Connors went in that direction. But, as time progressed, Teacher began to realize he was a collegiate standout and his mind began to wander to the tour. He would stay on at UCLA to help the Bruins to the NCAA team title his junior and senior years, but he would leave school about 16 units short of a degree, a situation he rectified by earning his diploma in economics when he retired from pro tennis in 1989: "Around my second year, when I won the Pac-8, I said to myself, 'You know, I'm kind of at the top of this college thing and I'm beating everybody so I should think about going pro. I mean, why not, what do I have to lose?' "

At 6-foot-3, the lanky Teacher thrived on fast-court surfaces where his serve and volley style was at its best. He would win eight career titles, reach 15 additional finals, and be among the top 10 in the world, topping out at No. 7 in October 1981. The tour was a very different animal in its pro infancy — paychecks lacked in the extra zero department — and facilities weren't state of the art: "We still had fun," he said.

Teacher's crowning achievement was becoming a Grand Slam champion by winning the 1980 Australian Open. Heading into Melbourne, Teacher had reached the final at the five previous tournaments he played: Los Angeles, Hong Kong, Taipei, Bangkok and then the Australian Open tune-up tournament in Sydney. What most people don't know is that Teacher nearly didn't play at the Australian Open that year, initially planning to fly back home to resolve a family matter.

Teacher had met and married fellow California player Kathy May, also a Top 10 player, when they were very young. May, who came from a very prominent background, decided to leave the tour early in the fall of 1980 but Brian was continuing to play. May also came from strong Jewish roots although she was raised in the Protestant faith. Her father, the late David May II, was a notable figure in the Los Angeles Jewish community as the heir of the family business — May Company Department Stores Co., which operated 324 stores in 31 states and the District of Columbia when he died in 1992. Her maternal step-grandfather Mervyn LeRoy, who she considered her grandpa, was a famous Hollywood director and the producer of "The Wizard of Oz," and also was Jewish.

"I was married kind of young at the time and it's kind of a funny story, and I don't think it's ever been publicized," said Teacher, starting to describe the circumstances behind his Australian Open victory. "We weren't getting along that well so it was right after my final match at Sydney when I called home and I said, 'I just lost and I had match point' and the first thing out of Kathy's mouth was she wanted a divorce. I said, 'What?' That's like crazy and we had just been talking about moving and starting a family. I thought about it, the Australian Open was supposed to start in two days and I was definitely playing the best tennis of my career and I was going to be seeded. But I said to myself, 'You know what, I think something is going on here, maybe there's another guy involved.'"

Convinced he would be unable to focus on playing, Teacher decided to pull out of the Australian Open and go home: "I actually called up (Australian Open tournament director) Colin Stubbs and pulled out of the draw. I told Colin I had hurt my back from all those finals in a row and he said, 'Too bad.'"

His bags packed and less than a half hour away from leaving his hotel room for the airport, Teacher received a call that changed his mind: "I got a phone call from Kathy's father, David, and he told me that it's not going to do you any good to come home right

Brian Teacher

now. There's too much stuff going on with Kathy so I shouldn't bother coming home. David told me, 'Why don't you just go to Hawaii, take a break.'"

Teacher thought about his father-in-law's advice but decided a solo Hawaiian vacation as his almost two-year-old marriage was on the rocks wouldn't be any fun: "I didn't think I'd have a good time in Hawaii so I might as well just stay and try to play this tournament. I called Colin Stubbs back four or five hours after my first call to him and said, 'Colin, you know what, I just went and got some acupuncture and it feels much better. Do you think you can let me back in the draw?' Colin said, 'You know Brian I can't do that, I just took you out of the draw and put somebody in, but I think somebody else is pulling out of the tournament so let me see what I can do, but you can't tell anybody because I'm not supposed to do this.'" In today's world, this could never happen, but back then Stubbs managed to sneak Teacher back into the competition.

The rest is history. In a draw that included marquee names such as Guillermo Vilas, Ivan Lendl, Jose Luis Clerc, Vitas Gerulaitis, Brian Gottfried and Yannick Noah, Teacher came through with the win, defeating surprise finalist Kim Warwick 7-5, 7-6, 6-3 in the final for the victory he describes as "meant to be." It should also be pointed out that Teacher is the last major champion that holds a university diploma, a further sign that playing college tennis fell out of style as players turned pro earlier.

Back when Teacher played, almost all the players competed in singles and doubles and Brian was no different. He won 16 doubles titles in his career with a variety of partners although he was often linked with fellow Californian Bruce Manson (also a Jewish player) with whom he won five titles.

Playing in a time when there were many prominent Jewish players on the tour, it was just an incidental fact if you happened to be of that faith. However, with a generic last name like Teacher it was hardly a given that fans were aware he was a member of the tribe. That fact became very clear at the 1980 U.S. Open when Teacher faced Israeli Shlomo Glickstein in the second round, a match that Brian won in five sets.

"I remember playing Shlomo at the U.S. Open and maybe people didn't realize I was Jewish," he said. "And here I'm an American and the whole crowd, they're going crazy for Shlomo. I guess, maybe, I should've said, 'Hey I'm Jewish, too.' I should have. I was all pissed off and I'm trying to focus and am all irritated. And besides that we were playing at that very back court at the back of Flushing Meadows where they had the hamburger stand and the whole time hamburger smoke was blowing in my face."

Teacher's marriage to Kathy May did dissolve, but Teacher's second marriage was a happier match and the couple have two daughters. He taught both to play tennis when they were little but neither had much interest in the game. Recently, Brian credits his oldest, Noelle, in awakening a little more of an interest in Judaism.

"I had a Bar Mitzvah," he noted. "I'm spiritually religious. I like the tradition. It's funny, but my older daughter is embracing the tradition much more than I am so she's kind of bringing me back to the fold."

Since his retirement from tennis, Teacher has undergone two hip replacements and suffers from osteoarthritis — he was diagnosed at 19 with arthritis, initially in his neck and spine. Despite the pain, Teacher remains active to combat the disease and does a lot of Vikram Yoga. For a long time, he traveled as a coach to other players — Andre Agassi, Greg Rusedski, Max Mirnyi, Jim Grabb, Richey Reneberg, Daniel Nestor, Mark Knowles — but nowadays operates the boutique Brian Teacher Tennis Academy close to his home in Southern California.

Teacher was enshrined in the ITA Hall of Fame, NCAA Tennis Hall of Fame and Southern California Jewish Sports Hall of Fame.

ALL I WANT IS SPAGHETTI
Michael Fishbach

It's not that Michael Fishbach was a major force to be reckoned with during his tenure on the men's pro tour. But in the late days of summer in 1977, this 22-year-old Long Islander courted international headlines. And even more than 30 years later, Fishbach's 15 minutes of fame still garners occasional attention.

So what did Fishbach do to create his long-lasting legacy? He delivered a one-two punch to Billy Martin and Stan Smith, respectively, as a qualifier at the 1977 U.S. Open. In the regular world of tennis, those two upsets would've been soon forgotten instead of recorded in tennis history. But those were matches that Fishbach won using a homemade spaghetti racket.

Fishbach grew up in tiny Great Neck, the town where F. Scott Fitzgerald spent some time living and for which he modeled West Egg, the fictionalized setting of The Great Gatsby. As soon as Fishbach arrived on the pro circuit after attending UC-Irvine, he quickly became known as a free spirit around the tour. One day when Fishbach was playing on the European swing, he saw 40-year-old Barry Phillips-Moore playing his matches with a curiosity of a racket, the original double-strung racket designed by Werner Fischer, a German horticulturist by trade and tennis junkie by hobby. Phillips-Moore, an Australian long beyond his heyday, was not swinging this odd racket, but he was knocking down wins he no longer should be posting.

The racket was just the kind of edgy tool of the trade that would captivate Fishbach's attention — it looked different, almost like something a novice weaver might produce and hope a veteran craftsman would approve. One thing it definitely accomplished was to cause opponents to want to pull the hair out of their head in frustration. The spaghetti racket made tennis balls do crazy things although it in no way enhanced a player's power. As Fishbach said in an August 2012 *New York Times Magazine* article, "Queens Was Burning Too," written by Michael Steinberger, "I had a lot of wrist and racket control. If players were ranked on the basis of ability to produce severe angles and drop shots, I would have been among the top players in the world."

Unfortunately, Fishbach's interest in getting a look at the odd racket was thwarted as Phillips-Moore guarded his secret weapon as if he was James Bond 007, on a grand mission. One day, however, while Fishbach was browsing in a camera store in Gstaad, Switzerland, he encountered a racket that very similarly resembled Phillips-Moore contraption. Fishbach's attempt to purchase the racket fell short — the camera store owner would not part with his possession. But he let Fishbach examine it closely enough to get a feel for how the stringing worked.

When he returned home to New York, Fishbach told his older brother, Peter, a former player and coach before joining the business world to eventually become a Senior Vice President at Philadelphia-based Advanta, all about the spaghetti racket. The brothers immediately set to work at stringing their own spaghetti racket. It took 30 hours or so to do — there's no sending

Michael Fishbach

out a racket for a quick stringing job when it came to the double-strung hammer — but in the end they combined various materials including nylon strings, plastic tubing and adhesive tape to fashion their version of the racket.

Ranked 200th in the world, Fishbach showed up with the racket to play the U.S. Open qualifying. Three matches won and he was into the 1977 U.S. Open main draw where the men's matches were best two-out-of-three sets until the quarterfinals. After taking care of Billy Martin 6-1, 7-5 in the first round, Fishbach moved on to face the incomparable Stan Smith, a former Wimbledon and U.S. Open champion, in the second round. He didn't just beat Smith; he pummeled him 6-0, 6-2, before going out to John Feaver in the third round.

A few weeks later, Ilie Nastase, who had lost to a spaghetti racket-wielding Frenchman Georges Goven at Paris in September 1977, showed up with a spaghetti racket of his own to play Guillermo Vilas. The Argentine, cruising on a 53-match winning streak, was so outraged at the unnatural shot making the racket produced that after playing two sets he forfeited the match as well as the winning streak.

Prior to the appearance of the spaghetti racket, the ITF had no rules set for what is a legal or illegal tennis racket. That all changed with this controversial new stick that took away any of the judgment an opponent normally could make on what type of shot was about to come back at them. It wasn't long after Fishbach and Nastase's use of the spaghetti racket that the ITF placed a temporary ban on the use of this new-fangled racket in October 1977. By June 1978, the spaghetti racket was forever outlawed in the game and nowadays there are rules and regulations as to what constitutes a legal racket design.

In today's world of tennis, while layered strings remains a violation, many players prefer synthetic strings that enhance the spin on a ball and help disguise ball bounces better than old-fashioned gut strings of the past. As Fishbach said to Steinberger in that *New York Times* article, "They banned the spaghetti racket, but they've been chasing it ever since."

After a decade playing pro tennis and reaching a career high of No. 47 in January 1978, Fishbach hung up his regulation rackets and retired from the game. Fishbach has gone on to have a successful career as a conservationist and is very involved in the preservation of whales.

MEET ME IN THE BOARD ROOM
Ilana Kloss

Ilana Kloss' dream of playing tennis at the highest level began when she was 11 years old and a ball girl at the South African Open. One of the players in the tournament agreed to hit a few balls with Kloss and told her father, Shlaim, he saw potential for a tennis future in his daughter. The comment didn't go unnoticed by Kloss, who includes the moment in her World Team Tennis bio: "When I heard that, I really began to dream about the possibilities and work toward being the best player I could be."

The words lingered in her mind and only a few years later she was fulfilling her potential as well as her dream. In 1972, Kloss won the Wimbledon junior girls' singles title. Two years later, the talented left-hander captured the 1974 U.S. Open junior girls' trophy. The stepping stones to a pro career were completed and she was ready to branch out.

As Kloss developed as a pro, it emerged that her legacy was going to be greatly defined by the doubles game. While she did attain a very respectable No. 19 career-high ranking in singles in 1976, that result was eclipsed by her No. 1 world ranking in doubles the same year.

It's not surprising that she was the best doubles player in 1976 considering she captured six titles that season. And the most important was winning the U.S. Open doubles title, teaming with frequent partner and fellow South African Linky Boshoff to defeat Olga Morozova and Virginia Wade 6-1, 6-4 in the final.

That was not, however, Kloss' first foray into a Grand Slam winner's circle. Earlier that same year, Kloss scored the French Open mixed doubles trophy with Australian Kim Warwick by her side. The two took a hard-fought final battle 5-7, 7-6, 6-2 over Boshoff and Colin Dowdeswell.

Kloss kept close to her Jewish roots when she took part in two Maccabiah Games, and left Israel a champion. In the summer of 1973, Ilana won gold in singles, doubles and mixed doubles. In 1977, she went home with gold in the women's doubles.

There's no denying, however, that Kloss' most impactful presence in the game is related to World Team Tennis.

Ilana was still in her teens — 18 to be exact — when she joined the Golden Gaters team in 1974. The franchise, with Kloss as part of the team, would reach the WTT Championships in 1975 and 1976, losing to the Pittsburgh Triangles and New York Sets, respectively.

That was the beginning of what has been a lifelong commitment to the team competition. She was with the Golden Gaters, then the Oakland Breakers (1981), the Los Angeles Strings (1982). In 1983, she coached the Chicago Fyre to the WTT Championship and was named the league's Coach of the Year. She then moved to be a player/coach for the Long Beach Breakers (1984) and Miami Beach Breakers (1985).

Kloss went on to take a political role related to WTT as the player liaison to the men's and women's tour. From there, she eventually moved into the executive offices of the league. In 1987, she was named the Vice President of WTT; in 1991 she moved up to Executive Director; and in 2001, she became the WTT Chief Executive Officer and Commissioner, a role she still maintains. In 2011, the *Sports Business Journal* recognized Kloss as a leading sports businesswomen in the game.

Ilana Kloss

In her bio on the World Team Tennis website, Kloss explains her dedication to World Team Tennis: "WTT is about both men and women competing together on a level playing field. Our vision is to grow tennis and make it a true team sport. With Mylan WTT, we are able to bring the best professional players to local communities where kids can see them working together as a team. That's an important inspirational message. Mylan WTT is also about giving communities a sense of ownership in tennis and a connection to our players. We provide a level of access and involvement fans generally can't get with other sports."

Kloss' life has been entwined both professionally and personally with Billie Jean King for the large majority of her adult life.

In business, it's all about World Team Tennis. King is the central figure of the team concept that she pushed into existence back in the 1970s. Kloss is the day-to-day executive dealing with every facet of the co-ed tour that runs in July during the U.S. summer.

As romantic partners, Ilana and Billie Jean have been together for 35 years. Ilana was attracted to Billie's way of opening up to everyone she encounters. Billie saw Ilana as organized and good company. As their good friend Elton John said on the PBS show "American Masters: Billie Jean King," "They are a twosome. They work brilliantly together."

While they still maintain an apartment in Chicago, the couple primarily reside in an Upper West Side apartment just a stone's throw away from New York's Museum of Natural History. As Billie has often said, "Ilana walks to work every day, if she doesn't run." The World Team Tennis offices are located on Broadway and 57th Street.

Kloss was elected to the International Jewish Sports Hall of Fame in 2010.

SHLOMO IN SLOMO
Shlomo Glickstein

Until Shlomo Glickstein came along, the country of Israel didn't really exist on the tennis map.

While one would think that the Mediterranean weather Israel enjoys would be ideally conducive to producing tennis players, back when Glickstein was a youngster, there wasn't much opportunity for talent to develop. Of course, tennis courts existed and hotel resorts had plenty of them for their guests visiting the Holy Land. And some clubs around the country had a few courts, but they were primarily reserved for members. So from the time Glickstein picked up a racket at 10 until he was about 16, he only played about twice a week.

Nevertheless, Glickstein, who would eventually forego his interest in basketball and soccer, would not be turned back from playing tennis. By age 12, Israel's national coach Ron Steele had taken notice of Shlomo's talent and would travel once a week to Glickstein's hometown of Ashkelon to help coach the promising youngster. Steele's effort paid off as Glickstein became a top-ranked junior and traveled internationally to play exclusive junior events such as the Orange Bowl in Miami.

Glickstein, however, couldn't just go about having a career in tennis — or go on to university — following his junior days. From age 18 to 21, he was obligated as an Israeli citizen to fulfill his compulsory military duty, eventually ranking as high as sergeant in the army. While his military superiors helped out by basing him near the Israel Tennis Center, where he could train during off hours, there's no denying that Shlomo fell behind his tennis contemporaries around the world. At one point, Shlomo pondered whether tennis was the ideal career path to pursue. But when his father, Moshe, the former chairman of the Israel Tennis Association's Youth Committee, passed away in 1978, Shlomo decided following a path in tennis would be the perfect way to honor his memory.

A latecomer to the tour, Glickstein didn't waste any time finding his place in the computer rankings, climbing from the high 200s to near 50 soon after turning pro in April 1979. In 1980, he won the first of his two career titles at the Hobart, Australia, tournament — his second title came in South Orange, New Jersey in 1981.

But it wasn't the Hobart victory that brought Glickstein attention. That honor came at his first career Wimbledon in 1980 when he upset the 35th-ranked Raul Ramirez. Israeli journalists were quick to compare Glickstein to the biblical Samson, who just so happened to also have come from Ashkelon. Never mind that Shlomo would lose to Bjorn Borg in the next round — even the Swede couldn't help but be impressed with Glickstein's amazing progress. "He has been doing very well. After all, he's been on the circuit only one year," said Borg. And Glickstein didn't leave Wimbledon empty-handed — he won the Wimbledon Plate event.

Glickstein remembered back to that Wimbledon when he spoke with Ari Louis, the host of the Louis Live Sports Radio Show on TLV1 at the end of 2013: "It was probably the most exciting tournament in my entire life that first Wimbledon. ... Playing Borg on the Centre Court at the beginning of my career gave me all the confidence I needed although I

Shlomo Glickstein

lost in three sets. I only have good memories of that match and from then on went on to have a great career. In those times, they used to play what they called The Plate, which was the consolation event for the first and second-round losers. I think I was the last winner of that event because after that they cancelled it. I have a very nice trophy, a very nice plate from that tournament and I still have it with me 33 years later."

Only two years into his career, Glickstein became the first Israeli to reach a Grand Slam quarterfinal at the 1981 Australian Open, losing to eventual finalist Steve Denton. At home, he was heralded as a hero when he became the first Israeli to ever win the men's singles title at the 1981 Maccabiah Games.

In 1981, Ivan Lendl said of Glickstein, "He has great anticipation. He always waits for the ball where the ball is coming. He looks as if he's going to move very slow, but he is really very fast. He always does the right thing." The No. 1-ranked Lendl would get his closest look at the Glickstein he described in 1981 when the 48th-ranked Israeli upset him in the first round of the 1983 Monte Carlo Open.

"My biggest win was probably beating Lendl," Glickstein said on Louis Live. "Maybe it was the best tennis I ever played."

By 1982, Glickstein attained a career-high ranking of No. 22. And in 1985, he partnered with Swede Hans Simonsson to reach the French Open doubles final, losing out on the title to the Aussie and Kiwi duo of Mark Edmondson and Kim Warwick.

Glickstein was dedicated to playing Davis Cup for his country, taking part in 24 ties from his first time playing in 1976. He still holds Israeli Davis Cup records for the most total wins at 44-22 and most singles wins at 31-13. In 1987, he was instrumental in Israel reaching the World Group quarterfinals.

After his playing career, Glickstein became the CEO of the Israel Tennis Association, the tennis governing body for tennis in the country.

FINDING A PLACE IN THE TOP 10
Eliot Teltscher

When one took a look at Eliot Teltscher on a tennis court, he certainly didn't come across as particularly threatening. At 5 feet, 10 inches tall and a spindly 150 pounds, it seemed as if one strong breeze would knock him over like a feather.

Of course, Teltscher wasn't the only guy out there in his generation that didn't quite have the most athletic build. John McEnroe was an inch taller and probably a few pounds heavier, but they appeared of the same mold.

Looks, however, can be deceiving and that was certainly the case when it came to Teltscher — and McEnroe. The California-born and bred Teltscher ended up being one of the best of his time, journeying to a career-high ranking of No. 6 in the spring of 1982.

While you wouldn't exactly say that Eliot was the most fabulous of athletes, he had some very important assets in tennis. When it came to his game, his premium weapon was a delicious one-handed backhand, which he handled with a simple fluidity.

But it was his head that delivered him to the top of the game. Teltscher was an intelligent thinker on the court, a headstrong and determined competitor. Eliot understood his strengths and even looking back years later he had little doubt about why he met with success on the court.

"I was just a baseline player," said Teltscher, reminiscing in a *Los Angeles Times* article from September 26, 1991. "I didn't have all that much of a game, but I just tried real hard. A lot of the guys played better than me, but I just tried harder."

The obstinate personality Eliot showed in the pros was developed at a very young age. He was the child of a Sabra mother, born in pre-state Israel Palestine, and a father who immigrated to Israel as a Holocaust survivor and joined the British military. By the time Teltscher was born, the family had relocated to Southern California.

Living in upscale Palos Verdes, Teltscher and his older sister, Judy, would join their parents at the Jack Kramer Tennis Club when they were children. By the time he was 9, Teltscher had taken up the sport. He'd often play against Judy and, in the lore of sibling rivalry as the younger brother, he was desperate to be better than his older sister.

It was at the Jack Kramer Tennis Club that Teltscher began working with the coaching maestro, Robert Lansdorp, a Dutchman with a great track record of superstar players he had a part in developing including Tracy Austin, Brian Teacher and eventually Pete Sampras, Maria Sharapova, Lindsay Davenport, and Anastasia Myskina, to name a few.

Almost immediately, Lansdorp saw that what Eliot brought to the table was a refusal to lose. Teltscher was stubborn and demanded winning results of himself.

"Since he was 10, 11 years old he was always so tenacious," said Lansdorp, in that same *Los Angeles Times* article from September 1991. "He's a fighter. He would run down everything. Every time you played the guy, you had a battle on your hands."

Teltscher would close out his life as a top 10-ranked junior with journeys to the Wimbledon and U.S. Open junior finals in 1977. At that Wimbledon, he shared a room with John McEnroe, who surprisingly qualified and journeyed all the way to the men's semifinals that year. As the story is told, the room they shared only had one bed so the two took turns having the bed or the floor for the night.

By 1978, Teltscher was off to UCLA to play tennis. He received All-American honors and was considered the second-best collegiate player in the country, right behind his Wimbledon roommate from the year before. At the NCAA Championships, it was believed that McEnroe, the best college player out of

Eliot Teltscher

Stanford, and Teltscher would vie for the prestigious NCAA singles title. But the anticipated final match never happened. Teltscher didn't live up to his end of the bargain, losing to North Carolina State's John Sadri in the quarterfinals. It was

Sadri who found himself in Eliot's supposed final spot against McEnroe, but he didn't have the goods to bypass the future world No. 1.

Teltscher didn't hang around at UCLA long enough to give the NCAA Championships a second try. Like McEnroe, he spent one year at college and then directed his effort to the pro tour. But his one-year stay was long enough for UCLA coach Glen Bassett to size up Eliot as a player with a personality akin to that of "The Little Engine That Could." Bassett said of Teltscher at the time: "Eliot believes in himself. He's very tough out there on the court."

It didn't take Teltscher very long to make his own noise once he joined the pros. His first year on the tour delivered a singles title in Hong Kong, the first of 10 career titles. He played on a number of U.S. Davis Cup teams, and posted career victories over McEnroe, Jose-Luis Clerc and Jose Higueras.

His best singles Grand Slam result was reaching the 1983 Australian Open quarterfinals, but along with fellow American Terry Moor, he attained a doubles final berth at the 1981 French Open, losing to Heinz Gunthardt and Balazs Taroczy 6-2, 7-6, 6-3. Two years later, however, the French Open would put Teltscher in the special class designated for Grand Slam champions. He teamed with fellow American Barbara Jordan to win the mixed doubles trophy 6-2, 6-3 over Americans Leslie Allen and Charles Strode. It's worth noting that, for a time, Teltscher dated Barbara's younger sister, Kathy, who was also a notable player.

Eventually, nerve problems in his right arm affected his ability to play at an optimum level and Eliot would call it quits following the 1988 season. He would go on to have a number of coaching positions. He worked as a personal coach with the likes of Pete Sampras, Justin Gimelstob, Jeff Tarango, and Taylor Dent. In the early 1990s, he coached the Pepperdine University men's team. And for a time he was one of the United States Tennis Association's national coaches.

In 2009, Teltscher was inducted into the International Jewish Sports Hall of Fame.

COULD'VE BEEN A CONTENDER
Van Winitsky

It's not easy being anointed a future star of the game, especially when it turns out that in the end a career didn't develop as hoped. That would be Van Winitsky's story.

A devilishly handsome guy, often referred to as a Tom Selleck lookalike, Winitsky came into notice as a promising junior. He was seen to have many advantages, starting with a power lefty serve and an all-around artistic game. In 1977, Winitsky gained notoriety as a top junior, winning the Wimbledon and U.S. Open junior boys' singles trophies by defeating fellow American Eliot Teltscher in both finals. That same year, he also won the prestigious USTA National Boy's 18 Championships at Kalamazoo, Michigan. And before all of those achievements, Winitsky had won the international junior Orange Bowl title on three occasions, including back-to-back wins in the 12s and 14s in 1971 and '72.

Winitsky had carved out a potential destiny of greatness for himself – at least everybody thought so. He came up through the junior ranks at the same time as fellow lefty John McEnroe - Winitsky being just 14 days younger than

McEnroe. In the juniors, the two were on par, or it could even be said that Winitsky was the better player than McEnroe. While McEnroe went off to Stanford, Winitsky attended UCLA, where he earned All-American honors.

Once they hit the pros, however, it was McEnroe who pulled away to become a superstar. And the three times they played in the pros, including a 1982 Wimbledon first round in which McEnroe was the defending champion, all belonged to McEnroe. Ahead of that Wimbledon match, Winitsky pointed to the shift in how their matches played out: "Up until the age

Van Winitsky

of 16, I could beat John. The last time we played was two years ago, and he won in three sets."

So what happened to Winitsky? He was hit in his prime with a shoulder injury that required surgery when he was 23. Not only could the 16-inch scar prevent Van from ever forgetting the injury, but his arm suffered an atrophied muscle. As much as he tried, he could never find the power he once had in his arm and often was in pain.

Winitsky attained a career-high singles ranking of No. 35 and won three titles — Hong Kong in 1981, Guaruja, Brazil and Hilton Head, South Carolina in 1982. In doubles, he achieved a career-high ranking of No. 7 and won nine titles, and reached the 1983 U.S. Open doubles final with Fritz Buehning.

Upon retirement, Winitsky moved around a great deal and tried a variety of different careers. He pursued modeling, frequently coached, and even volunteered as a Tennis Director at the Boys and Girls Club of Greenwich, Connecticut. He also has done his share of playing — and meeting with success — on the international senior tour.

In 2009, years after his retirement, the Beth David Congregation, a conservative synagogue in Miami, invited Winitsky to be one of its local Jewish athlete honorees at a special ceremony timed to coincide with the world-class Sony Open in the city. Van showed up with his dad, Manny, who was once one of the elite senior players in the country. Both Winitskys were clearly moved by the moment as Van shyly listened to the list of his achievements that resulted in his being chosen for recognition.

THE CHATTERBOX WITH SOMETHING IMPORTANT TO SAY
Brad Gilbert

The prevailing opinion from anyone who knows Brad Gilbert is that he must talk in his sleep. If you're wondering why, the answer is pretty simple — Brad is a chatterbox. The California native is absolutely never at a loss for words and when it comes to talking tennis — or all sports, for that matter— it's worth listening because he's naturally gifted in providing sports analysis. It's no wonder that Gilbert has been a highly successful professional player, coach and ESPN TV commentator — he is a self-proclaimed sports junkie.

Oh, and let's not forget that he also has written two books: *Winning Ugly*, which is a description of his playing style, and *I've Got Your Back*. The premise behind *Winning Ugly* is it's a book dedicated to winning matches from a mind-game perspective, a talent in which Gilbert excelled. In *I've Got Your Back*, Gilbert offers insight into the tour, a winning approach to coaching, and why great players rise up to achieve their "personal best."

While he was attending the 2013 Orange Bowl Junior Championships at the behest of the USTA, Gilbert was asked whether he's flattered to be considered one of the great minds in the game. He smiled at the notion: "I have to be honest with you I just feel like I compete," Brad said. "I like to compete, and the great thing about tennis is two men enter the court and one man leaves. You get the opportunity every time you play to compete and have a chance to win."

Gilbert was born on August 9, 1961 in Oakland, California and has an older brother Barry Jr. and older sister Dana. It's likely that being the baby in the family explains his ability to speak frequently and quickly to get his point across, a trait of many younger siblings.

Tennis became a focus for the three Gilbert children when the sports-minded Barry Sr. discovered the game.

"You know, to the best of my knowledge, I think when my older brother was like 6 or 7, for some reason my dad bought a couple of rackets for like a dollar at a flea market or won them," Brad said. "So they went out to play tennis a couple of times and then my dad got every book on tennis and he just said in the next few days after 'that's it, we're playing tennis.' He had never played tennis in his life. He didn't know anything about it. So we all just started playing. I started playing at 3."

Brad's brother, Barry Jr., had an ATP ranking of No. 390. His sister, Dana, played on the WTA Tour for five years after attending UCLA with her best Grand Slam outing being a fourth-round finish at the 1982 French Open.

Brad paints a picture of his dad as a guy who can become totally consumed by something that catches his interest and tennis clearly did: "My dad was incredibly passionate about a few things. He's a dying breed of a Jewish guy who thinks the Democrats are like Communists. He likes Republican politics and he loves tennis," Brad said with a bit of a laugh.

Brad Gilbert

I remember distinctly it was early in Brad's tennis career — and early in my career as a sportswriter when I was sitting in this rickety two-story lean-to media center at the Longwood Cricket Club in Boston, Mass. It was a popular clay court event played after Wimbledon in July. Brad was just coming onto the stadium court and the phone in the press box started to ring incessantly, but the press officer was not there at the time. It became so annoying that I decided to pick it up and it was Barry Sr. — he knew Brad was on the court, the match was not being televised and he wanted a point-by-point description. When I explained that I was one of the journalists and was working but I'd tell the press officer or ATP Tour media person that he had called when they got back, he prevailed upon me to provide the details. I have to say I did sit there and give him a point-by-point of the match. I remember that he was rather desperately persuasive.

Brad definitely shares an infatuation with the game similar to his dad. And his competitive nature motivated him to the top of the tennis charts.

Brad attended Foothill Junior College in Los Altos, Calif., from 1980 to 1982 and it was there where he met Tom Chivington, the school's tennis coach, who would become Brad's guru throughout his career. Not only did Tom often travel with Brad, but so did his wife, Georgie. The Chivingtons were, without a doubt, a second family for Brad. While at Foothill, Brad won the California Junior College singles championship and the U.S. Amateur Hardcourt Championships held in Cleveland. In 1981, Brad was selected to the Junior Davis Cup team that traveled the American summer circuit with Steve Stefanki, the older brother of Larry Stefanki, as the team coach.

Gilbert also would take part in the 1981 Maccabiah Games in Israel, where he teamed with Jon Levine to win the gold medal in doubles. It seemed natural that Gilbert would participate in the Maccabiah Games — the Jewish Olympics — as he was raised with a nod to being Jewish and did have a Bar Mitzvah. Brad's wife, Kim, is not Jewish but they've incorporated both religions lightly into raising their three children.

"I don't come from a pseudo-religious family," Gilbert said. "We went to a Conservative temple, maybe we would go on the High Holidays. My grandmother kept kosher, but that was about it. If you ask me if I'm Jewish, I'm Jewish. We light the candles on Hanukkah at home and I know of other things. But we have a bit of both (religions) in the house."

While Gilbert points to the successful Jewish players during the time period he played, including his good friend Aaron Krickstein, as well as Brian Gottfried, Brian Teacher, Harold Solomon, Eliot Teltscher, Jay Berger, Amos

Mansdorf, and Jim Grabb, he believes their being Jewish had little impact on their careers: "The one thing about tennis is that when you walk through the gate it doesn't matter what religion you are, what color you are — nobody cares. That's the great thing about tennis, that when you're playing a match, it's just about a chance to compete and beat someone who is trying to beat you."

After the summer of 1981, Gilbert returned to Foothill, but the following year he transferred to Pepperdine University where Allen Fox, a former Jewish player and former U.S. Davis Cupper from the amateur days, was the coach. Brad would be an All-American at Pepperdine and reached the 1982 NCAA singles final, losing to Mike Leach of Michigan. With Brad's assistance, Pepperdine posted an impressive 23-5 record for the season.

In the end, however, Gilbert would end his college days to turn pro after his junior year and start traveling on the tour. He would spend nine of his first 10 years on tour ranked in the top 10, reaching a career high of No. 4 in January 1990. Gilbert would win 20 career titles, was a valued member of the U.S. Davis Cup team, reached the quarterfinals at the U.S. Open in 1987 and Wimbledon in 1990, and won the 1988 Olympic singles bronze medal in Seoul, South Korea. And he achieved remarkable victories over many of the greats of the game — Boris Becker, Stefan Edberg, Pete Sampras, Jim Courier, John McEnroe, and even Jimmy Connors.

Still, Gilbert is one of those guys that is always hard on himself. So even when asked to remember back to what the highlight of his career was he offered it with a glass half-empty instead of half-full mentality; "Hey, it's just great I got to play for 13 1/2 years and loved every minute of it," he said. "Probably my biggest high and low came at the same tournament. Getting a bronze medal, but I always think that maybe I got ahead of myself in thinking it should've been the gold because there was a great opportunity with Edberg losing. There was some opportunities but I lost to my teammate Tim Mayotte, so it was probably the high of my career and the low because I thought I had a chance to win it."

To this day, you'll find tennis insiders and fans scratching their head at the success Gilbert had in the game. His big weapon wasn't a serve, a volley, or anything like that. In fact, when it came to his strokes he didn't have a big weapon — he had a fine serve, a finer return-of-serve, good groundstrokes, and decent volleys — but nothing stood out as breathtaking. What Gilbert had beyond speedy court coverage was his uncanny ability to frustrate an opponent. He relentlessly fought for every last point. He was adept in taking players out of their own game and many thought he cleverly lulled opponents into an ineffectual daze.

When he retired from tennis in 1995 having earned over $5.5 million in prize money, Brad was not ready to walk away from the game he loved. Toward the end of his career — in 1994 — he started to switch gears by becoming Andre Agassi's coach. His alliance with Andre lasted until January 2002 and during their time together Andre won six major singles titles and once again became the No. 1 player in the world. The next year, Gilbert started working with Andy Roddick and it was during their partnership that Roddick won his lone major title at the 2003 U.S. Open.

Gilbert also had coaching stints with Andy Murray, Alex Bogdanovic, Sam Querrey, and Kei Nishikori, the latter who was Brad's son Zach's roommate at the Nick Bollettieri Academy.

A guy who is clearly capable of multitasking, Gilbert is also one of the faces of ESPN's tennis coverage and, to be sure, he keeps the commentary lively and insightful. Tennis addicts listening in to Brad dissect a match consider it pure heaven as well as a teaching lecture on how to play the best tennis possible.

If Brad's friend Aaron Krickstein tells it like it is — and there's no doubt he is doing so — the older Brad still is as enthusiastic as ever and most resembles the energizer bunny in everything he does: "I've stayed at Brad's house several times and a few times we've gotten up early," Krickstein said, laughing. "I'm not a bad morning person but I like to have some quiet time and coffee. I like to read the paper and digest everything and have a cup of coffee. But that's not the way it is when Brad is around. He's going to tell me everything before I read it from the get go - from 7 a.m. he's going to be going non-stop. And I'm like, 'Take a breath, Brad, I'm just like waking up here. That's his personality — you've gotta love Brad for who he is.'

And who Brad happens to be is a guy totally content with the life he leads.

"I've been really fortunate," Gilbert said. "Since I'm 20 — I'm 52 now — so 32 years later I'm still involved in tennis and I still love it."

A WOMAN OF MANY HATS
Elise Burgin

When Elise Burgin was a little girl back in Baltimore, she qualified as one of the neighborhood tomboys. Mom made a concerted effort to expose Elise to diversified opportunities. But in the end, the cute little girl's predilection was to be a jock.

"I took three years of ballet, but I'd much rather be out playing tackle football with the boys," Burgin remembered. "I started at tennis when I was 8 and played my first tournaments at 9. We belonged to a club and I did everything that my older brother (Harold) did and he was playing tennis. I swam competitively — I was a very good swimmer, but once I started hitting tennis balls I just went insane. It was love at first strike, and I would just hit on the backboard at our club for hours. For me, that was heaven."

Nowadays, Burgin, a spirited and funny adult who could easily thrive doing standup comedy, laughs when she thinks back to the Jewish-oriented mantra she'd repeatedly uttered to herself when competing in matches as a child.

"I would be out on the court, and I'm so young, and I'm playing these matches and fighting my guts out and I would tell myself, 'You can do it, you're one of the Chosen people,'" said Burgin, cracking herself up at the memory. "Here I was, like 9 years old, and I was thinking I'm one of the Chosen people. I had heard someone say that and at the time I didn't even know what we were chosen for. I didn't have a great understanding of what it meant, and I wouldn't say it out loud, but I'd tell myself that and it would spur me on."

As it turned out, Burgin, the daughter of a prominent doctor, had good reason to need a mantra boost. One wouldn't think of Baltimore, Maryland, as a Mecca of tennis, but back when Burgin was growing up, she was one of a trio of talented young girls from the neighborhood who would go on to play professionally. The other two were Pam Shriver, just a few months younger than Burgin, and Andrea Leand, who was two years her junior.

"It's pretty amazing when you think about it," said Burgin, of Baltimore producing tennis phenoms. "I don't know that something like that would happen again. It was interesting. Andrea and I, our first tennis teacher was the same. Andrea, Pam and I, we all lived within a couple of miles from each other. I went to public school — if we had all gone to public school we always would've been in the same school, but Pam and Andrea both went to private school."

Maybe even more surprising, two of the three — Burgin and Leand — were both of the Jewish faith.

Born in January 1964, Leand, whose father was also a physician, made a big splash as an amateur in 1981. Only 17 years old, she reached the Wimbledon junior semifinals, won the Maccabiah singles and mixed doubles titles, and journeyed to the round of 16 of the women's main draw at the U.S. Open. In September of that year, and despite her achievements of the summer, Leand went off to Princeton University. But she would only stay a year before venturing out to the pros. She spent a few years on tour, briefly holding a career-high ranking of No. 12, but couldn't keep the momentum going. In 1985, she returned to Princeton to finish her degree in psychology and then rejoined the tour in 1989. She kept to it for a few years, but by the early 1990s had traded in her tennis racket for a computer and for awhile became a working journalist covering the pro tour.

For Burgin, however, it was the same-aged Shriver with whom she bonded closely — to this day she refers to Pam as her best friend — and with whom she enjoyed an intense childhood tennis rivalry.

At the beginning, they both played the same brand of backcourt tennis and it was Burgin who had the advantage: "When we were kids we'd just stand back there and see who could moon ball higher. We played these matches — she was always a couple of heads taller than me — but we'd just pushed each other to death. Mentally, we'd

Elise Burgin

play these very competitive, long matches in the summer, but we didn't see each other often in the winter."

And that was the way it was until that summer they became preteens. Shriver had begun training with a new coach, the Australian Don Candy, and the moon balls were immediate collateral damage of the new alliance. The first time Burgin faced Shriver that summer she was stunned into disbelief — Shriver was a different — and vastly improved — competitor.

"Oh my God, she came out serving and volleying and I almost had a heart attack," Burgin said. "We've been playing for how many years these ridiculous long matches and now she was serving and volleying. Her changing her game taught me how to hit passing shots, that was the positive. But it was a shock. Life changed when Pam started serving and volleying. In our pushing matches, I always won them. When she started serving and volleying, I won a couple and never won again." Indeed, Shriver won all three of their professional encounters.

By the time Burgin was ready to head to Stanford for college, Shriver had already turned pro and as a 16-year-old had lost in the 1978 U.S. Open final to Chris Evert. Always level-headed, Burgin knew she had the choice to turn pro, but also understood to do so really wasn't an option.

"In my parents' minds, their Jewish kid wasn't turning pro, that wasn't happening," Burgin admitted. "Out of my generation there were a couple of players who were slam dunks to turn pro like Pam and Tracy (Austin). I could've turned pro and I knew I was going to have a professional career, but at what level I didn't know. But I knew I was not Tracy and not Pam. And in my mind, and my parents' minds, there was no question I was first going to college."

By the summer between Burgin's junior and senior year she put up great results as an amateur playing the season's pro tournaments, which found her fielding constant questions as to whether she was going back to school. On track to graduate the following spring with a major in print journalism, she decided it would be foolhardy not to go back to Stanford. It ended up being a very wise decision as a back injury surfaced and kept her off the court from September through April. She began playing just in time to win the 1984 NCAA doubles title with teammate Linda Gates.

When Burgin looks back to her pro career, she quickly isolates the highlights, starting with being selected to play Fed Cup and Wightman Cup for the United States. She also considers the few times she played with Shriver forever memories, most especially when they teamed to win the 1987 Washington, D.C., title, the event they considered their home tournament.

But, undoubtedly, one of her funniest tour tales was becoming tongue-tied when Martina Navratilova approached her to play doubles at the 1985 Houston tournament the next week. Burgin had just been contemplating skipping Houston with a hamstring injury. In the end, she realized you don't turn down the best player in the world. Not only did the duo win the doubles title, but Burgin had a great singles week as well, beating two top-10 players — Zina Garrison in the quarterfinals and Manuela Maleeva-Fragniere in the semifinals — before losing to Navratilova 6-4, 6-1 in the final.

"I'll tell you the story of Martina asking me to play doubles — it's actually very funny," said Burgin, always in good delivery form. "I tore my hamstring and I was just miserable and I was thinking, 'I'm not playing Houston next week.' I'm standing there and Martina comes up to me and says, 'Hey, do you want to play doubles next week?' As Martina told the story it was the first time in her life that she asked somebody to play doubles and they didn't give her an immediate answer. I kind of looked at her in shock and I think I just kind of walked away. It was amazing how quickly my hamstring healed — when I came to my senses that Martina had just asked me to play doubles. I said, 'OK, I guess I'm going.' And the irony of that is that I ended up having one of the best singles weeks of my career."

One of the most frustrating experiences of Burgin's career was when she lost her spot on the 1988 Olympic team to Chris Evert. At first, the 33-year-old Evert was concerned about the dates of her upcoming wedding to second husband, Andy Mill, as well as the quality of the security in Seoul. But then Evert decided she wanted to play, which pushed the 26-year-old Burgin off the team. Burgin didn't take offense and was a guest at Evert's wedding just days after the announcement that it would be Evert, not Burgin, representing the U.S. in Seoul.

From the moment she joined the tour, Burgin raised her hand to become politically active in the game. She served for many years on the WTA Player Board, including as an officer, and was a player representative on the WTA Council. She remembered as a child when Billie Jean King made headlines for being the first female athlete to earn $100,000 in a year and marveled when she mimicked that achievement years later. Nonetheless, as much as $100,000 seemed like a lot of money, equal prize money to the men wasn't on the table. It was under the watch of Burgin and her fellow board members that the fight for equal prize money commenced and she's proud to have been an instrumental force in the growth of the game.

All good things must come to an end and Burgin believes that everyone has a sixth sense about when it's time to retire. For her, that decision came when she was 31. She was ready to discover her second career. After careful thought she decided to put her degree to good use and signed on at a mid-market local TV station in Harrisburg, Pennsylvania, as a reporting intern. Eventually, she became the affiliate's sportscaster, a position she kept at for a number of years. Nowadays, she continues her broadcast involvement by working for places such as the Tennis Channel.

Having spent much of her adult life traveling the world for weeks on end, there were many times Burgin recalls it being advisable to keep the fact you were Jewish under the radar. That said, there's no denying that Burgin's Jewish identity has been, and continues to be, an essential part of her life.

Although she remained in Harrisburg even after her position at the ABC affiliate ended, it is close enough to Baltimore where her brother, Harold, an attorney, lives with his family. And as has always been tradition within her entire extended Baltimore family, Burgin maintains an active membership at Temple Har Sinai, the oldest ongoing Reform congregation in the United States and the place where she was confirmed as a child.

"That's where we've always gone — that's where we've belonged," Burgin said. "It's always been an important thing to me to belong to the congregation because we (Jews) are a small minority and I want to still see us flourish."

GRABBING A PIECE OF HISTORY
Jim Grabb

For two-time Grand Slam doubles champion Jim Grabb, a defining moment that joined his tennis life with his Jewish identity came years after he set down his racket following the 2000 season.

The occasion took place 13 years after he retired at the Wingate Institute in Netanya, Israel, in July 2013. The Wingate campus is the home of the International Jewish Sports Hall of Fame and Grabb was being inducted as one of the 2013 honorees along with 19 others. The IJSHF enshrinements take place on a quadrennial basis and are timed to coincide with the Maccabiah Games — the Jewish Olympics — which are always held the year following the traditional Summer Olympics.

For Grabb, the 2013 trip to Israel was a three-generation family experience. His mother, Lola, and his two young daughters ages 10 and 8 were in tow. And the focus was on more than just Jim's entrance into the Hall of Fame. His wife, Sarah Stenn, won Maccabiah gold in the 40-49 age bracket in the half-marathon category.

"The one thing that comes to my mind that is more toward the Jewish trajectory is when I was inducted into the International Jewish Sports Hall of Fame," Grabb explained. "When I collected my thoughts to say a few words there, I kind of made a joke that tennis and my Judaism did not peacefully coexist when I was a youngster. I would be stuck in Sunday school watching the clock waiting for the bell to ring and the chance to leave and go play tennis at the racket club. And then over the years there was so much travel, and although I had many friends who were not Jewish, Judaism was something, maybe it's a little dramatic (to say), that kind of created home from one place to the next, one country to the next. And not exclusively, but the people that in meaningful amounts I gravitated to on the tour were Jewish, whether it was Brad Gilbert, Amos Mansdorf, and Brian Teacher coached me a little bit. So, there was a sense of Judaism (offering a feeling) like home. I remember going to an old synagogue in Rhode Island or High Holy Day services in Australia, which also offered a common theme. And I wasn't that religious and never really was that religious."

Within the Jewish community, Grabb is known as a Jewban. His family history originated in Eastern Europe, but when his ancestors fled Europe as many Jews did, they landed in Cuba where his parents' generation grew up. Eventually, the Grabbs ended up in Tucson, Arizona, where his father, Sam, was a urologist. The Grand Canyon State was where Grabb was born and raised.

When the time came, Grabb went off to Stanford University, an institution known for its high-powered education and as a tennis school of distinction. While an

All-American at Stanford, where he pursued a degree in economics, Grabb captained the Cardinal team that won the 1986 NCAA title and reached the 1985 semifinals. In 1985, he reached the NCAA singles semifinals as well. And in 1986, Grabb won the prestigious Rafael Osuna Award, an honor pre-

Jim Grabb

sented by college coaches to a college player who has shown good sportsmanship with a competitive spirit, and who was a valuable asset to the team.

During his pro career, Grabb was ranked No. 1 in doubles in 1989 and 1993. A notable serve-and-volleyer, he teamed with Patrick McEnroe to capture the 1989 French Open doubles trophy and partnered with Richey Reneberg to win the 1992 U.S. Open title. Along with Reneberg, Grabb also played in the 1992 Wimbledon final, losing to John McEnroe and Michael Stich in a final that went to 19-17 in the fifth set and that lasted a couple of days when delayed by darkness. The Grabb-Reneberg duo turned the tables on McEnroe-Stich in a five-set semifinal win en route to their winning the 1992 U.S. Open title later that summer.

In all, Grabb won 23 doubles titles in 50 finals played. In singles, he achieved a career-high ranking of No. 24 in 1990, and captured two singles titles – in Seoul in 1987 beating Andre Agassi for the trophy, and in Taipei in 1992. A member of the 1993 U.S. Davis Cup team, Grabb posted wins over some heavyweight competition in his career, including Agassi, Michael Chang, Stefan Edberg, Ivan Lendl and Mats Wilander.

It's always curious as to what reflections a player comes up with when asked to think back over their career. For Grabb, what many would imagine to be an inconsequential 2-6, 6-2, 7-6 (4), 6-3 first round victory over Frenchman Jean-Philippe Fleurian at the French Open marked a momentous occasion.

"My best memories from the tour, two would be winning the French Open and the U.S. Open in doubles, which are two that are obvious, self-evident," said Grabb, who then laughed as he told of another tennis recollection. "But you know, I won one match in my entire career in singles at Roland Garros and I remember feeling really, really satisfied after winning that first-round match. I walked into the locker room thrusting my arms up in the air, partly as a joke and partly for real."

When his playing days were over, Grabb briefly helped with a tennis program at the Tennis Center of College Park outside of Washington, D.C. But on the whole, Grabb was ready to take his life in a new direction. He earned Certified Financial Analyst credentials and went into finance. Eventually, Grabb ended up working side-by-side again with Reneberg. For a few years the two had neighboring offices in New York at Taconic Capital Advisors LP, a hedge fund company.

"I was so burnt from traveling so I had no problem switching gears," Grabb admitted. "My two different roles were sitting in the office and interfacing with existing investors or to go out and drum up new business, and I had no interest in getting on a plane and doing that."

While tennis is no longer the main focus of Grabb's life he does make a family trek from his home in Long Island to the U.S. Open, where he reached the fourth round in 1989 — his best career singles Grand Slam result — just for a little walk down memory lane.

MUCH MORE THAN THE MAN
WITH THOSE BABY BLUES
Martin Jaite

When Martin Jaite showed up on the men's tour in 1983, he had more than a few girls swooning. This good-looking, blonde haired, blue-eyed tennis player was a Paul Newman lookalike. The two even share a Jewish heritage, although for Newman it was just his father who was born into the religion. And like Newman, Jaite's baby blues, trained in your direction, only added to his charm, making him hard to miss.

Born in Buenos Aires, Argentina, Jaite was a product of an international childhood. His parents — his mother was a psychologist and his father a psychoanalyst — moved from Argentina to Barcelona, Spain, when he was 11 years old. He would excel in junior tennis in both countries and seven years later he would win the 1982 Spanish National Championships and the Banana Bowl junior title in South America. He would also reach the French Open junior boys' semifinals.

No matter where he was living Jaite was a sports-oriented youngster. Competing was a natural fit for Jaite, who when he was 5 years old won a swimming meet at his Buenos Aires Club. He was happy about the win but infuriated when the club neglected to give him his medal. He also participated in soccer and handball at school.

Not surprisingly, both countries believed in Jaite's potential and were interested in his playing under their flag. At first, he tried to respect both nations as they both played a part in his development. When he was 19, Jaite returned to Argentina with his mother and even then was reluctant to accept an offer to

Martin Jaite

align himself with the Argentine Davis Cup team. But the country of his birth and current residency eventually prevailed and Jaite began competing as an Argentine.

While Jaite had little power in his game and could hardly blow an opponent off a court, he did have his own weapons to rely on. He was a consistent player, a smart tactician, and his prime fitness enabled him to speedily cover the court. And his topspin backhand, one of the tougher shots in the game, certainly helped his defensive skills prevail.

In 1985, two years after he started playing on the pro tour, Jaite could really believe he'd arrived on the scene. It was summer and the tour was at its stop in Indianapolis, Indiana. Jaite scored a surprisingly lopsided 6-0, 6-1 win over fellow Argentine and his boyhood idol, Guillermo Vilas. It was the first of their three career meetings that would end with Jaite holding a 2-1 career edge. Despite securing that round-of-16 victory, Jaite's comments following the match were in deference to the Argentine maestro who inspired many generations of South American players to take up the game: ''We have to give thanks to Vilas for all the courts and tournaments we have in Argentina,'' Jaite said. ''It was because of him.''

No matter how successful Jaite became in the sport, he always had the good graces to remember that if not for Vilas, tennis might never have become as popular as it did in Argentina, or South America.

In 1990, Jaite would officially join the top 10 club — weighing in at No. 10 in July of that year — thereby becoming the sixth South American man to rank in that elite group since the advent of computer rankings in 1973. The other players to achieve that feat ahead of him were: fellow Argentines Vilas, Jose Luis Clerc and Alberto Mancini, Victor Pecci of Paraguay and Andres Gomes of Ecuador. During the year, he became one of the best in the business, Jaite again called attention to the role Vilas played in Argentine tennis: "There are two eras in Argentine tennis: the 'Pre-Vilas' era and the 'Post-Vilas' era. Before Vilas, tennis in my country was only for the high society. Now, it is very popular — the second most popular sport next to soccer. We owe that to Guillermo."

One year after his 1985 Indianapolis victory over Vilas, Jaite was playing in New York ahead of the French Open. It was at that 1986 Shearson Lehman Brothers Tournament of Champions in Forest Hills that he would secure another prominent scalp in beating 18-year-old reigning Wimbledon champion Boris Becker 6-2, 7-6 (3). Jaite, a specialist on the clay, managed to overcome what he referred to as "a nervous head" to prevent Becker from winning their quarterfinal.

For the Argentine with those Paul Newman blue eyes it was a moment to remember for a lifetime, even better than his previous win over Vilas: ''This is the best day in my life. I think Boris is a better player than me, and if we played 10 matches, he would win 9 or 8.'…He played with pressure, and I had nothing to lose."

His reward for beating Becker was a second career outing against Vilas in the semifinals. It was hard to forget that Vilas had won his 1977 U.S. Open title in the famed horseshoe stadium at Forest Hills in which the semifinals would take place. And Vilas certainly felt he still had ownership of the arena, beating Jaite 6-3, 6-3 to journey to the finals.

The future for Jaite would hold other major wins, including over two of the talented Swedish major winners Mats Wilander and Stefan Edberg. There would also be 12 career singles titles and a French Open quarterfinal showing. He would compete in the 1988 Seoul Olympics, losing to Brad Gilbert, the eventual bronze medalist, in the quarterfinals.

Jaite's days of competing came to a close after the 1993 season, but he didn't leave the sport he loved behind. Instead he moved into the business end of the game, becoming the tournament director of the Buenos Aires ATP event, Challenger and Future-level tournaments. He also spent time coaching fellow Argentine David Nalbandian, who achieved a world ranking of No. 3 and was the 2002 Wimbledon finalist.

And in 2012, Jaite, who played in 17 Davis Cup ties over a nine-year period, fulfilled a personal dream when he became Argentina's Davis Cup captain: "This is a dream I've had since I stopped playing tennis," said Jaite of taking over the Davis Cup efforts.

BETTER LATE THAN NEVER
Amos Mansdorf

Unlike many famous tennis players who have a racket put in their hands practically before they're even walking, Amos Mansdorf had to wait his turn to play.

His father, Jacob, a chemical engineer, and mother, Era, a headmistress of a school, would take little Amos with them to the Herzyliya Country Club in Israel as a very young child. He was there to take advantage of the swimming pool, but the lone tennis court at the place immediately captured his imagination. His interest, however, just met with frustration.

"When I was very young we were at the swimming pool at a club that had one tennis court there and I was always watching the people playing," said Mansdorf, chatting in the players' lounge at the 2014 French Open. "I was about 5, 6 at the time and they wouldn't let me play. They said I was too young and that kids don't play at that age, and it's no good for the back."

He might not have been allowed to step foot on that tennis court, but that denial only heightened Mansdorf's wish to play. It was back at a time when there weren't many tennis courts in the small Mediterranean nation with ideal tennis weather, and those that existed were usually located at tourist resorts.

His mother knew how much he wanted to play, so when she saw an ad in the paper when he was 9 years old that the Tel Aviv University Tennis Club was looking for talented athletic kids to join their program, she took Amos for a tryout. Unfortunately, he didn't pass the audition and was crushed. Again, he was left on the outside looking in.

Mansdorf's fate for the start of his life in tennis, however, was just one year away. In 1976, the Israel Tennis Center, being funded by wealthy Jews from places such as South Africa, the United States, Britain and Canada, was launched. Eventually, there would be multiple Israel Tennis Center complexes, but the first — and flagship — of the ITC was practically built in Mansdorf's backyard. He was from Ramat Hasharon, a suburb of Tel Aviv, and a nearby strawberry patch in the town saw tennis courts blossom instead of succulent fruit.

Initially, Mansdorf, even stubborn as a 10-year-old, refused to be persuaded to give tennis another chance. He'd been turned away from the sport twice and didn't want to suffer another disappointment. Amos' resolve eventually weakened and the door to his future opened.

"In 1976, they opened the Israel Tennis Center and I lived in Ramat Hasharon where they opened the first center," Mansdorf said. "So my mother said I should go and try. So I said, 'Look mom, they said I'm no good' and I didn't want to go, but then my (older) sister got accepted. So I said, 'If she got accepted, maybe I have a chance.' I went there and they scouted the better kids and I met the coach who coached me for many, many years and that's how I started."

Mansdorf came to tennis later than most do, but the constant Israeli sunshine enabled him to make up for lost time. He spent hours on the court demanding himself to improve.

By 1983, Mansdorf turned pro. He would go on to have a successful career that produced six titles, appearances in the 1984 and '88 Olympics, and allowed him to be a loyal member of the Israeli Davis Cup team.

On the court, Mansdorf was a feisty competitor with no glaring weaknesses and no overwhelming weapon when it came to his strokes. But like so many players, he was smart, cunning and determined, and putting those components together can be powerful ammunition. He also developed a reputation of being a prickly sort on the court.

Amos Mansdorf

When chatting with Amos at the French Open, I tactfully suggested he was considered a "spirited" player. His reaction — immediate laughter: "Spirited? You mean temperamental, don't you? Yes, Yes, Yes, Yes, but I was not the worst. But I did everything with my heart and emotions and it's good to be spirited."

When one is of a minority group and a "spirited" personality, it could prove to be a recipe to developing some uncomfortable situations. While Mansdorf admits that being mercurial left him a target to occasional criticism, none of it took on an anti-Semitic tone. While that might be true, there is at least one incident in his career where a comment made in relation to Mansdorf by a fellow player to a third party would definitely have anti-Semitic undertones.

The setting was Flushing Meadows, New York, the home of the U.S. Open, in 1989. Mansdorf was playing Yannick Noah in a barn-burner of a third-round match that spanned two days — rain at 5-5, 0-30 with Mansdorf serving ended play on Friday night. Eventually, when they reconvened on Saturday the match went in Noah's favor 3-6, 3-6, 7-6, 7-5, 6-2.

The encounter, however, was not that friendly skirmish kind of engagement. Tempers flared and Noah initially refused Mansdorf's handshake at the end of the match. While the Frenchman eventually yielded to custom and shook hands, the two had a lengthy and heated exchange at the net.

As in any argument, there were two sides to the story.

Noah claimed Mansdorf verbally attacked his mom, sister and girlfriend watching courtside from the friends' box: "During the match (Friday) night, Amos went to my family and insulted them. I told him I didn't want to shake his hand because of what he told my family."

Mansdorf claimed that Noah's family members were the cause of the problem by trying to disrupt his concentration when serving and he admittedly retaliated with some unkind words in their direction: "His family — his sister, in particular — was intimidating me on purpose. She saw she was getting to me, and she kept on doing it. I lost a big point, and I just said something. I apologize for that publicly. But his family, after watching so much tennis, should know how to behave, and intimidating me on purpose is not the right behavior, for sure."

When the two left the court following the match conclusion on Saturday, the fans booed Noah, undoubtedly a reaction to his initially refusing to shake Mansdorf's hand at the net. Noah stopped to talk to French television and Filip Bondy of the *New York Daily News* was standing nearby and his fluency in French came in handy that day. "Did you see the shape of their noses?" Bondy reported was Noah's comments to the French TV, suggesting the fans all possessed ethnically Jewish noses as a reason why they favored Mansdorf. Years later, in a May 2011 article in the *Daily News*, Bondy retold the incident in relation to Noah's son, Joachim, an NBA star with the Chicago Bulls, making a politically incorrect statement.

The good times on tour lasted for more than a decade until Mansdorf met an adversary he couldn't beat: Chronic Fatigue Syndrome. The doctors told him this was a battle that was going to get the better of him and not vice versa. So at 30 years old he put down his rackets and moved on. "I did one semester at university after I retired but I was already a businessman," said Mansdorf. "I was in the diamond business for many years but I stopped in 2011." And where did he go afterward? Back to his tennis roots, traveling the tour as a coach to players such as Israel's top woman Shahar Pe'er.

When it comes to Judaism, the Mansdorfs promoted a cultural rather than religious perspective within the family.

Their beliefs came directly from his four grandparents, all of whom immigrated to Israel from Poland.

"We come from what is called social Zionism background," Mansdorf said. "The grandparents came from Europe many, many years ago in the '20s, the last century. They were pioneers on both sides so they didn't really look at being religious."

The concept of a worldwide Jewish community came across for Mansdorf as he traveled the world. At many tour stops, particularly in North America, France and Great Britain, fellow Jews came out and offered their cheers and a sense of family to a stranger in a strange land, to the many Jewish players on tour.

"I always felt like I was at home in the U.S," Mansdorf confirmed. "We had very big support from the Jewish community in North America, a lot of places — in France, here, there's always been a big Jewish community to come and support us. In London also, but especially in North America, which was very, very nice."

THE MAN WITH THE BACK-SCRATCH SERVE
Jay Berger

It sounds very cliched to say, but nonetheless is very true: Trying to catch up with Jay Berger is like trying to hit a moving target. Jay is here, there and everywhere, which is not that surprising considering that since 2008 he's served as the USTA Head of Men's Tennis. Trying to develop talent is no easy or part-time responsibility.

It was never that Berger wasn't amenable to chat about himself, his life in tennis, and his relationship to Judiasm. It's just he's one guy trying to be in a multitude of places at the same time. Just watching him traverse a Grand Slam tournament with American players — pros and juniors alike — on courts peppered around the grounds is dizzying to the observer.

Finally, during a relatively mundane work week at the USTA's Boca Raton training facility, Jay phoned, first offering apologies for being so hard to pin down, and then with the good news that he had some time to talk - right then and there.

"You're in a car," the question was posed, but not needed since the background noise betrayed Berger's whereabouts. He laughed, "Yes." The response: "Perfect, you're a captive audience then." Jay patiently waited as the tape system was turned on and then spent some quality time telling his story.

Jay was born in Fort Dix, New Jersey, but relocated with his family to South Florida where Jay grew up and initially facilitated his own interest in tennis.

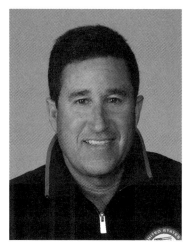

Jay Berger

"I started playing tennis on my seventh birthday," said Berger, the son of a dentist. "I got $10 from my grandmother and I went out to Walmart and bought an Emerson racket. I started by hitting balls in the street with my dad."

Berger quickly upgraded from the road in front of his house to a tennis court, playing at Center Court, a club in Sunrise, Fla., where standout doubles star Robert Seguso also played. A half year into owning that Emerson racket and Jay was taking a once-a-week tennis lesson and by eight he was starting to play 10-and-under tournaments.

"I was dropped off at the courts at eight in the morning and picked up at five o'clock," said Berger, thinking about how he developed as a youngster. "I would just try to find people to play with. I'd just hang out at the courts at the club all day. I'd play with anyone I could find."

Back in Berger's time, there were so many quality juniors in South Florida alone that a player had all the competition they needed to improve while living a more traditional childhood. Part of Jay's normal childhood routine was attending Hebrew School and being Bar Mitzvah'ed. Of growing up, Berger said, "Judiasm was definitely part of my life and who I was." He remembered that his dad donated money to the Israel Tennis Center. Nowadays, however, Berger says, "Not so much," when asked if he's active within the Jewish community. His wife, Nadia, isn't Jewish and they haven't raised their four children in the religion.

"There was definitely a sense of who the other players were who were Jewish and I think there probably still is," Berger admitted. "You know, when I see (Israeli tennis player) Dudi Sela I think he knows who I am and I know who he is — there's definitely some recognition."

From the time Berger was 12-years-old to throughout his pro career his main coach was Jorge Paris. But he also was fortunate enough from his mid-teens to pick the brains of tour players Brian Gottfried and Harold Solomon. Solomon would frequently hit with Berger, but it was Gottfried who would become a vital mentor and coach. Besides for Berger, Gottfried worked at the same time with Aaron Krickstein, Jimmy Arias and Greg Holmes.

"I was lucky at 16 to start training with Brian Gottfried," Berger said. "Brian was a huge influence in my life, my pro career. I couldn't have a better transition to the pros than with someone like Brian, who was such a consummate professional. In a different way, Harold was also an influence."

In 1985, Berger made quite a splash in the juniors, winning the USTA Boys' 18s Clay Court and USTA Boys' 18s Hardcourt titles. The latter, more commonly known as Kalamazoo, comes with a special prize to the victor every year - a wildcard into the upcoming U.S. Open.

Still an amateur, the No. 730th-ranked Berger, who had only ever played one pro tournament prior to the U.S. Open — losing a first-round match in Boston that summer — made great value of that U.S. Open wildcard. He journeyed to the fourth round, where he fell in four sets to Yannick Noah. To reach that fourth round, however, Berger upset Brian Teacher, the 1980 Australian Open champion, in a four-setter in the third round. The big joke about Berger at that U.S. Open was that this unknown junior and his family had to keep checking back into the swank St. Moritz Hotel on Central Park South every time he'd win his match. No other Kalamazoo champion has fared better as Berger did at that U.S. Open in the Open Era.

In today's world, Berger would've probably taken that fourth-round appearance as a sign he was ready for the real world: the pros. But in those days, juniors went on to college and that's exactly what Berger did. He enrolled at Clemson University, where he spent two years and received All-American honors before joining the pro tour.

During his career, Berger won three titles (Buenos Aires in 1986, Sao Paulo in 1988 and Charleston in 1989). He ended the 1989 season with a year-end best ranking of No. 10, enjoying a career-high ranking of No. 7 in April of 1990. His best results at the Grand Slams was reaching two quarterfinals — at the 1989 French and U.S. Opens. He also represented the United States in Davis Cup, winning both singles matches he played.

"For me, the highlight was playing Davis Cup, without a doubt," Berger said. "That's something I always dreamed of being part of and is one of my greatest memories. Obviously, making it to the Top 10 was something I'm not sure I ever thought I'd be able to do. Getting to the quarterfinals of a couple of Grand Slams would be some of my highlights. And getting to the semifinals at the Lipton (Key Biscayne) at home in front of friends and family was exciting."

During his career, Berger claimed a number of victories against top players, including Mats Wilander, Pete Sampras, Michael Chang and Boris Becker. In fact, when he upset Becker 6-1, 6-1 in the Indian Wells third round, en route to the semifinals, it would turn out to be the worst defeat Becker would suffer during his stellar career.

"Really, when I look back on my career I think the thing that is nice is that I did everything I could to be the best player I could become," Berger said. "I was known by my peers to be a great competitor, somebody who was pretty fierce on the court. You know, it's great to be able to look back and have no regrets in the way I went about my tennis and I think that's what it's all about."

Berger would be the first to admit that although he was a top 10 guy his American compatriots, such as Pete Sampras and Andre Agassi, kept him from being a major focal point in the game. However, there is one notable, quirky style to his game that many fans remember clearly. Berger had a unique service motion where he did away with the normal backswing motion of a serve. When he got in position to serve, his starting point was with the racket located behind his back — almost as if he was using it as a back scratcher.

"My serve developed — the first time I ever used it I was 16-years-old and I was playing the 16-and-unders at Kalamazoo," Berger said. "I was going to graduate high school a little bit ahead so that was the year that college coaches were going to be looking to recruit me because I was going to graduate at 17. In my first round match I pulled a muscle very badly — my chest muscles — and the only way I could've continued the tournament was to continue serving in a half motion. I served some of the best tennis I ever served.

"That was the first time I ever used that serve," Berger continued. "When I went to college my first year I was having a lot of shoulder issues and I also wasn't serving that great - it was probably the weakest part of my game. So I just decided to try the serve again and it just worked better for me so I stuck with it and never went back."

Upon his retirement, Berger went into coaching and spent some time as a coach at the University of Miami. In 2003, he joined the USTA national coaching staff, working to help current players and assist in identifying talent for the future. Berger believed his path after playing the pros was to pursue coaching as it would fulfill his desire to give back to the game he loved.

"I find it extremely satisfying at times, sometimes not as satisfying, but overall I really enjoy what I do," Berger said. "I do love learning about tennis. I enjoy trying to become as good as I can as a coach. I don't feel like I go to work every day. I feel like I get to follow my passion."

THE RABBIS' GRANDSON MOST FAMOUS FOR A LOSS
Aaron Krickstein

If Aaron Krickstein's father, Herb, hadn't parted with family tradition, it's entirely possible Aaron Krickstein would've been a rabbi and not a tennis player.

Herb Krickstein was interested in taking a different direction than his father and grandfather. He was very athletic, played tennis in high school, but it was baseball that really captured his attention and he tried out for his beloved (Detroit) Tigers. But reality set in — baseball had little earning potential — so instead, Aaron's father set off to medical school, eventually becoming a pathologist.

"I come from a long line of rabbis until my dad broke the chain," said Krickstein, sitting in his office at the elegant gated St. Andrews Country Club where he has served as the Director of Tennis for the past 14 years. "I didn't know my grandfather Joseph that well, he died when I was 3. He was a rabbi and my great grandfather Aaron was a rabbi, too. It wasn't like we were ever Kosher or went to synagogue every weekend, but we certainly followed the traditions. Jewish heritage and the tradition were certainly important within the family."

Aaron Krickstein was born in Ann Arbor, Michigan on August 2, 1967, the youngest of four children, and the only son of Herb and Evelyn Krickstein. All four Krickstein kids played tennis and were nationally-ranked juniors. But only Aaron had the desire and perseverance necessary to make the game the focus of his life.

"Tennis is a tough sport and it's not for everybody," Aaron said. "There's a winner and a loser and you can't hide from it. Kids often don't want that pressure."

Raised in Grosse Pointe Woods, Michigan, a beautiful suburb of Detroit, Aaron learned to play at the country club where his family had a membership. He excelled to the point where he needed to branch out for coaching, and at ages 14 and 15 he would go twice a month to southwest Florida to work with famed coach Nick Bollettieri. At 16, Aaron moved full-time to the academy where he could have regular sparring sessions with Jimmy Arias, Andre Agassi, Jim Courier, David Wheaton, and occasionally with Brad Gilbert when he was in town. To this day, Arias and Gilbert are two of his closest friends.

For Krickstein, the Bollettieri experience was nothing but a positive for the five years he used the academy as his home base. The only bad moment he can remember was when one of the coaches was a little aggressive in preaching the value of Christian doctrine. Aaron called his father and explained he was uncomfortable with what the coach was doing. Herb Krickstein placed a call to Nick and told him that Aaron would have to leave the academy if the coach ever approached Aaron again.

"I had a great experience at Nick's," Aaron said. "Nick is who he is and he helped me a lot in a lot of ways. You know, he may not be the greatest coach for the x's and o's, but he was a great motivator. He really helped me to make the transition from the juniors to the pros. He was a fun and a positive guy to be around and

Aaron Krickstein

he was just a good friend for my time there."

There were those who were impressed with Krickstein when at 16 he won the U.S. National Boys' 18 Championships. But that achievement paled in comparison to when, at 16 years, 2 months, and 13 days old, he became the youngest player in history to win an official Grand Prix tournament title in Tel Aviv, Israel in 1983. That moment still remains one of his three most favorite memories of his career: "Of course, winning in Israel as my first tournament and winning the next year as well, I think that was kind of special with my heritage and tradition and everything," he said. "Winning there as a Jewish American was pretty cool, especially at 16."

Playing Davis Cup also was a highlight for Krickstein, although he clearly understood his place in the pecking order of the team. He played on five U.S. Davis Cup teams — two in Europe, two in South America and one in Asia — for a 6-4 record in the competition: "I would say playing

Davis Cup, even though I never got to play a home match," said Krickstein, when asked about his favorite memories. "I was always the guinea pig for the road because, for whatever reason, when the draw came out that way the others didn't want the tough venues. So I got thrown to the wolves. I had some tough losses to (Boris) Becker and (Victor) Pecci in the fifth match on the road. They were tough tasks to win, tough mentally and physically. I felt the weight of thinking I let the team down. But I really enjoyed playing Davis Cup."

His other favorite memory was how well he did at the U.S. Open, reaching the semifinals in 1989, quarterfinals in 1988 and two additional fourth-round finishes.

Nevertheless, it is not Krickstein's winning moments at the U.S. Open that he is known for around the world. Krickstein is the one guy in the tennis world who is forever linked to a match he lost. It was 1991 and the 24-year-old Krickstein played a fourth-round match against Jimmy Connors on Connors' 39th birthday. Despite their age difference, Connors was a friend and someone he often sought out as a practice buddy. Most of Connors' peers were long retired but not Jimmy. In a riveting match, Connors won in a fifth-set tiebreak. It was a particularly heartbreaking loss considering that Krickstein served for the match at 5-3 in the fifth set — a forehand return sailed long destroying that opportunity. There also was the fact that it was Labor Day, there was a large crowd that Jimmy was pumping up with his usual antics, not to mention that he was doing a good job of intimidating the linespeople and the umpire. The match would be one for the ages and one that would become historic as the go-to programming whenever the U.S. Open would be in rain delay in the future. No matter how many times they show that match, the outcome never changes — Aaron walks off the loser — and none of the commentators even bothered to mention that in the first round he dismantled Andre Agassi.

Krickstein is not only a realist, he's actually a really bright guy with a very self-deprecating sense of humor. So while there's a part of him that would prefer to be remembered for what he did achieve in the game — a successful 13-year career, a career high ranking of No. 6 in 1990, and nine career titles — he is willing to turn the negative of losing that match into a positive.

Aaron and I have lived in the same town for many years — Boca Raton — and have known each other since he started playing at 16. These days, we see each other on occasion, most often at a local restaurant or when I'll go over to St. Andrews to chat with him about some story or other I'm writing. Quite a number of years ago, I asked him whether he minded being famous for the match he lost. At the time, he told me, 'not really.' When I went to see him in January 2014 for this book, I asked him that same exact question to see whether he had any change of heart. "Whether I do or I don't, it doesn't matter," he said, 22 years after the match. "A lot of people recognize me and associate me with that match, which is fine. I mean, to be honest, in the beginning it kind of bothered me but at a certain point it does and doesn't. Real tennis people know that I played and had a good career. But the casual fan would know me from that match based on how many times it has been played. Maybe a lot of people in this new era wouldn't know me if that match wasn't played. So from that perspective, it's kind of a nice thing." Then Krickstein laughed, before continuing on with the ultimate conclusion, "Hey, I never beat him of the seven times we played so it was just another one, it just so happened to be a big one. I certainly wouldn't be as famous if I had won that match, we all know that."

During the fall of 2013, that match again became a focus in the sports world. As part of its documentary series "30 for 30," ESPN used Connors and that match as a story line. Interestingly, when ESPN debuted the film, it was Aaron who showed up at the New York opening and worked the crowd. Jimmy was nowhere in sight. No sooner than the documentary finished, my nephew Michael H. Weber, the co-screenwriter of "500 Days of Summer" and "The Spectacular Now," who attended the screening, texted me to say the film had a real bombshell moment.

Since playing that U.S. Open classic, Krickstein said he's not encountered or spoken with Connors. That said, Aaron says it really isn't as dramatic as it seems that he and Jimmy haven't had contact: "We just haven't talked," Aaron said. "It's not like I don't like him or he doesn't like me. It's just our paths have never crossed and it's not like I really reached out to him since and, obviously, he hasn't with me. It is what it is. But, of course, it's a film, so it made for a good story because I think that a lot of people didn't know. One time I saw him when I was at the Open in 2004 and we were going to cross paths but I got sidetracked by someone and I looked up when I was done with my conversation and he was gone."

When Aaron finally decided that injuries had taken too big a toll on his body, and after playing three tournaments in 1996 — the Australian Open, Philadelphia and Miami — he announced his retirement. From that point, he spent four years primarily taking time off. He learned how to scuba dive, started to play golf well enough to become a scratch golfer, and tinkered with a saltwater aquarium business. That was all well and good, but it didn't sit very well with the always highly-motivated Herb Krickstein: "I remember my dad saying to me, 'What? Are you going to stay retired for the rest of your life? You've been playing golf for four years.' I was doing the aquarium thing, having fun with it and making a little bit of money. But my dad didn't look at that as an income or something to be doing."

In that conversation, it wasn't as if Herb didn't already have a plan for his son, one that Aaron's late sister, Kathy, also was pushing him to pursue. The St. Andrews Country Club in Boca Raton, where Aaron's parents, as well as Kathy, lived, was looking for a Director of Tennis. Both were urging Aaron to return to tennis and take the job. Nevertheless, Aaron wasn't convinced that it was his calling: "I don't know if I'd say I didn't want to do it, but I wasn't sure if this would fit me or anything that had to do with having a responsibility and answering to someone and not being your own boss," Aaron admitted. "As a tennis player growing up, your whole life you're your own boss, right? You decide what you want to do, when you want to do it, how you want to do it, and so when the situation came up here I was like, 'Hmmm, three weeks vacation. I have to like come in and have responsibilities. It was just like a big shock to me. Experience-wise, the whole thing scared me, which I think was understandable, knowing that I'd never done anything like that."

Eventually, after giving it some thought, Aaron decided he'd give it a shot. But he laughed when revealing, "I had the over-under at probably six months of whether or not I was going to make it to six months or not — that was probably the betting line. And here we are — it's pretty amazing."

Much to Aaron's surprise, the job was a "really good fit." He believes that his knowing the club well — "a mostly Jewish club" is how he describes it — helped in the adjustment. As an added benefit, it was at the club that Aaron met his second wife, Bianca, who was St. Andrews Membership Director and Director of PR. He previously had a short marriage to Terri Goldfine, the sister of his one-time coach, Dean Goldfine.

Life has been good to Aaron, but there have been some personal hard times that he has had to get through in recent years.

First, his older sister, Kathy Krickstein Pressel, passed away from an aggressive form of breast cancer in September 2003. Aaron said that when the diagnosis came, his father knew right away that there wasn't much hope that Kathy would survive. Kathy Pressel left behind three children, including her eldest daughter, Morgan, the well-known LPGA golfer, who, like Aaron, had Herb Krickstein as a coach: "He tried Morgan in tennis but when he brought her out to hit for the first time she had lead feet," Aaron said of his niece. "She was lazy, wouldn't run after the ball. In tennis, you have to have happy feet — if you don't want to move, you're not going to be good at tennis because it's a game of motion."

One year after his sister, Kathy, passed away in 2003, while Aaron was playing in the U.S. Open senior event, and life was feeling perfect with a beautiful 10-month-old daughter Jade to dote on, his wife was diagnosed with gestational trophoblastic cancer. The disease develops in the uterus when a woman is pregnant and by the time Bianca was diagnosed, the cancer had spread to her liver, adrenal glands and both lungs through the blood stream. Bianca was one of the lucky ones. She underwent weeks of intensive chemotherapy with a mix of five different chemo drugs at Sloan Kettering in New York. Today, Bianca is healthy and cured, and after waiting the three-year period to make sure she was cancer-free, the Kricksteins were given the green light to get pregnant. Son, Joseph, five years younger than Jade, soon joined the family.

While Aaron works in tennis, his involvement is no longer with the elite pro game. Nevertheless, he does keep on top of what's going on and worries about what the tour will be like in 10 years. At the moment he isn't seeing — or hearing about — any future American stars ready to emerge in the game. What he does know about is the demands being a great player puts on an individual. As they say, hindsight is 20-20 and that does lead to one regret: "Looking back I wish I would've enjoyed some things more," he said. "I think most tennis players would tell you that. Sometimes when you're in the moment and young, you don't put things in perspective. I saw the Eiffel Tower, but I didn't take it all in. You're only thinking about winning, that's your only objective, getting better and winning."

THE SMASHING SMASHNOVA –
THE BEST NAME IN TENNIS

Anna Smashnova

From the minute that Anna Smashnova arrived on the tennis scene as a talented junior, her name garnered immediate attention. After all, there hardly was a more perfect name for a tennis player than Smashnova, considering the smash is one powerful tennis shot.

The irony of Anna being called Smashnova is that the smash was certainly not a weapon in this baseliner's tennis arsenal. The diminutive 5-foot-2 Minsk, Belarus-born, Israeli citizen, Smashnova hung her reputation on precision not power, consistency and court coverage instead of flash and splash, and mental toughness rather than big weapons. If there was one shot of Smashnova's that was of particular note, it was her one-handed backhand, a rarity in today's world where the two-fisted backhand reigns supreme.

Indeed, when in 2002 Smashnova became the first Israeli to ever earn a berth in the prestigious year-end $3-million WTA Championship, fellow player Serena Williams had this to say about the endurance of her colleague to *Tennis*

Week magazine: "(Smashnova) doesn't hit a powerful ball. But she'll probably tire you to death or run you to the point where you just can't run anymore then she'll probably come up with winners in the third set."

Smashnova started play-ing tennis at age 6 primarily because a tennis facility was located near her home in Minsk. She quickly showed off her athletic talent and was considered the best girl player in the Soviet Union. Two years prior to the Soviet Union breaking up into 15 separate countries in December 1991, Smashnova won the 1989 Soviet Union

Anna Smashnova

Youth Championship title at age 14. That victory changed the course of Smashnova's life.

In 1990, Freddy Krivine, one of the founders of the Israel Tennis Centers, extended an invitation to Smashnova and her family to come to Israel. The Smashnovas packed their belongings and immigrated to the homeland. Anna started to play under the Israeli flag, and in 1991, on the clay courts she favored, became the French Open junior girls' champion.

Smashnova embraced life as an Israeli. She trained at one of the Israel Tennis Center's state-of-the-art complexes and graduated from the American International High School near Tel Aviv in 1995. She was capably fluent in Russian,

English and Hebrew. She fulfilled her mandatory Israeli Army service by 1997.

Smashnova began her pro career in 1994. To this day, Smashnova's career-high No. 15 ranking on the WTA computer in February 2003 is the best of any Israeli woman in history. As evidence of her impressive start on the tour, *Tennis Magazine* named Smashnova its 1994 Rookie of the Year.

Despite the accolades, it took Smashnova until the 1999 Tashkent, Uzbekistan, tournament to win the first of her 12 career WTA titles, although she won six ITF-level tournaments prior to that. Amazingly, Smashnova won titles in her first 12 WTA final appearances with her last title coming at the 2006 Budapest, Hungary, tournament. It was only after that Budapest victory that Smashnova suffered her lone WTA final loss to American Meghann Shaughnessy at Forest Hills, N.Y. in 2006.

Certainly her best pro year was in 2002 when she won four titles — Auckland, Canberra, Vienna, Shanghai — and defeated 11 of the Top 20 players she faced, including wins over Belgians Justine Henin and Kim Clijsters.

Smashnova also had a distinguished Fed Cup career representing Israel. In fact, on the list of Fed Cup players who've competed at the most ties in history, Smashnova is tied in second place with fellow Israeli Tzipora Obziler — both competed in 61 Fed Cup ties with Smashnova having a 43-30 total wins record and Obziler coming in with 51-39. Only Luxembourg's Anne Kremer played more ties at 74 with a 61-57 win-loss record.

Where Smashnova didn't really excel as a pro was at the Grand Slams. Her best showing was at the French Open, reaching the fourth round in 1995 and 1998. From the time she turned pro in 1994 through 2003, Smashnova lost in the first round of 20 Grand Slam events. Despite that statistic, Smashnova told the *Jerusalem Post* in a Nov. 21, 2003 article that she didn't subscribe to any theory that she was cursed at the majors: "I don't really think that one can talk about a jinx. I am looking forward to playing the majors in 2004 and am confident that I will be able to play my best tennis at the Slams next year." Unfortunately, 2004 didn't bring great Grand Slam results either — she reached the second round at the Australian, third round at the French and then lost in the first round at Wimbledon and the U.S. Open.

Interestingly, despite her lack of success at the majors, Smashnova decided to end her career at a Grand Slam — Wimbledon in 2007. In 13 Wimbledon main draw appearances, Smashnova only advanced beyond the first round twice: in 1994, where she reached the second round in her debut, and in 2000, when she reached the third round. In her final Wimbledon — and her final career match — Smashnova went down 6-0, 6-0 to Martina Muller of Germany in the first round.

THE BEST QUOTE IN TENNIS
Justin Gimelstob

If Justin Gimelstob is anything, he's an independent thinker, which is why he doesn't quite buy into the conventional axiom that one's Jewishness is linked to one's mother's heritage. And for a good personal reason.

Gimelstob, you see, is the middle child from a mixed marriage. His mother, Patricia Ann, a former teacher, comes from a Catholic background. His father, Barry, the Chief Executive Officer of Financial Benefits and Research Group, a New Jersey-based insurance company, hails from a Jewish family. Their three sons — Joshua, Justin and Russell — were raised with a bent toward the traditional from both religions. His maternal grandmother was a "significant" part of his life and he attended church for Catholic holidays. He also attended Hebrew School but wasn't Bar Mitzvah'ed — one of his brothers went through the ritual for 13-year-olds — and Justin himself attended many Bar Mitzvah bashes. Throughout his youth, he attended the academically elite private school, The Newark Academy in Livingston, New Jersey, where many of the students also were Jewish.

So with that kind of healthy exposure to both religions, how does Gimelstob as an adult identify himself from a religious perspective? It took him about a nanosecond to respond as he stood outside a Tennis Channel cubicle at the 2014 French Open: "Jewish," said Gimelstob, quickly.

He went on to explain why he leans toward his Jewish roots: "I just view it more culturally. I know that technically it follows your mother's side. I was subject to and had access to both religions and also I don't view it as that concrete. I have a very Jewish name. I believe the whole concept of religion is how people view it. I view it as more faith-based, and more culturally based, and more heritage-based. And I felt a strong cultural Jewish connection and I think a big part of that is from my sporting background, from the fact that because my name was Jewish and there aren't that many Jewish athletes to root for, that I got a lot of support from the Jewish community. And I feel like I identified with that and was identified with that. I connect to that bond as well. It was that kind of 'we need to stick together; we need to support each other.' "

That said, Gimelstob followed in his parents' footsteps in marrying outside the Jewish faith. His wife, Cary Sinnott, is a psychotherapist in private practice. They were married in a dual religious Protestant-Jewish ceremony in May 2012 and have committed to exposing their infant son, Brandon, born in late 2013, to both religions. When Brandon's first holidays came around in December, they lit the candles on the menorah they received as a wedding present, and they also celebrated Christmas.

During his tennis career, Gimelstob was a standout as a junior. He won national titles in three age groups: the Easter Bowl 14s in 1991, the Easter Bowl 16s in 1993 and the U.S. 18s at Kalamazoo in 1995. By the time he was ready to head off to UCLA for college he had already played at the 1995 U.S. Open courtesy of a wild card extended as a prize for

Justin Gimelstob

his Kalamazoo victory. It was his first Grand Slam main draw, he was ranked No. 1,154 in the world and he upset the No. 65-ranked David Prinosil in the first round.

For some players, that U.S. Open victory might have steered them away from college. But not for Gimelstob and not for his education-oriented family. So off to UCLA he went. During his two years at college, he met with success on the tennis courts, winning the 1996 NCAA doubles title with teammate Srdjan Muskatirovic and also helped the Bruins to the 1996 NCAA team finals. But even more impressive, Justin was a star in the classroom, too, maintaining a perfect 4.0 GPA.

It was after two years completed at UCLA that Gimelstob decided it was time to set off on his world travels on the professional circuit. If it was up to his parents, he probably would've stayed put and finished his degree. There was no economically compelling reason for Gimelstob to have to go out and earn a living; the family had considerable financial means. But while Justin liked college life and learning, he was aching to play at the highest level against the very best.

Indeed, Gimelstob, who reached a career-high singles ranking of No. 63, had some impressive career milestone wins, posting upsets over the likes of a number of major champions: Andre Agassi, Michael Chang, Lleyton Hewitt, Petr Korda, Gustavo Kuerten and Patrick Rafter. His best overall showing in the singles realm was reaching the final in Newport, Rhode Island in 2006.

"At the end of the day, I look at my career and I got to play in every great stadium in the world against some of the greatest players of all time," said Gimelstob, proudly. "I had a 5-0 record in five-set matches at the U.S. Open and I'm very proud of that. You know, it all just becomes a blur. It all just becomes facts and figures and what stays with you is the fact that I got a chance for a long time to travel the world playing a sport, and now I still get to travel the world making a living being involved in the sport."

In the big picture, it was in the doubles arena where Gimelstob garnered his most notable achievements. He won 13 doubles trophies and was ranked as high as No. 17 in the tandem game. And it was via mixed doubles that Gimelstob became a two-time major champion. In 1998, he teamed with newcomer Venus Williams to win back-to-back mixed doubles titles at the Australian and French Opens.

When asked how he ended up playing with Williams, Gimelstob set the scene and put the victories into perspective. "That was completely random. Actually, people don't believe this — early on in her career she was with Reebok and I used to be with Reebok when I was on the national team. At that point, she wasn't the Venus that she became. She had never won a tournament. When we walked on the court to play the Australian Open final she told me it was the first title she was going to win if we won. She didn't play junior tournaments and at that point she had never won a professional tournament. So when we won the title it was the first pro tournament she ever won. But even back then you could tell she was someone special."

In retirement, Gimelstob has been able to evaluate the value of his Grand Slam mixed doubles success in a more prominent context: "It was ironic. At the time when I was winning them, it wasn't a huge focal point. Probably, in retrospect, it's a great thing to have on the resume and to be a Grand Slam champion is great. It was an interesting time in my life. You don't know — you don't have the wealth of information and the understanding of all the things going on — you're just trying to go out there and play. Obviously, to be a Grand Slam champion forever is nice, but at that stage, I was focused on trying to create a career for myself in singles and doubles and mixed doubles was kind of an afterthought. I just happened to be better at doubles than singles, but singles was always my priority."

From the minute Gimelstob arrived on the scene, he became known as one of the most quotable players. He's just never at a loss for words and quite often his thoughts are clever and cheeky. For instance, when he won that U.S. Open wild card by virtue of his Kalamazoo victory, Justin saw the glass as half-full: "I'm only seven matches away from my first Grand Slam title," he quipped. In 1998, when Gimelstob lost to Andre Agassi at the Los Angles tournament, which was held on the UCLA courts where he played college tennis, he joked, "This is my house; I'm just leasing it to Andre."

As is the case for many outspoken individuals it took Justin some time to learn that a broadcasting personality often needs to keep their personal opinions to themselves. Once he made that adjustment, Justin became a popular announcer. He capably explains the nuances of the game, discusses what a player is doing right and wrong, and offers an insider glimpse to the tour, much to the delight of those watching.

Gimelstob's always been drawn to multitasking, and continues to be that guy. Not only has he turned into a well-received broadcaster, but he remains a powerful political voice in the sport,. He first started getting involved in the organization of the game when as a player he served as an ATP Player Council member. In June 2008, as a former player, he was first elected to be an ATP Player Board Representative for the Americas region, a role he continues to hold.

"I think at the heart of anything you get involved in, it's because you think you can help," Gimelstob said. "Obviously, that's an underlying theme. But it's a little arrogant and presumptuous to assume that you can. But I'm very proud of what we've done on behalf of the players and the tour."

Another project that Gimelstob set out to accomplish once he put down his racket was completing his college degree. Some might wonder why he believed this an essential priority considering he quickly paved a path to a successful post-player career. But his reasoning makes perfect sense.

"I said I would do it, and I don't like not finishing things," he said, simply. "I told my parents when I turned pro, I would do it. I now have a son and I'm sure I'll stress education, and if he's a wise- aleck like me, I'm sure he'll say you dropped out of college. So I want to finish. I think it's important to finish things you start and to keep your commitments."

DOUBLING DOWN FOR ISRAEL
Jonathan Erlich/Andy Ram

I was having a conversation with Nick Imison, second in command of the ITF's communication department, at a Davis Cup tie when he inquired how I was doing on writing my book. Nick had been a star helping me get a number of interviews lined up, including with Jonathan (Yoni) Erlich and Andy Ram. When I told him that I was up to crafting the chapter on Israel's Grand Slam doubles champions, Nick smiled and said, "They are so lovely — so nice."

Nick then said, "Let me tell you a great story about Jonathan and Andy." Of course, I was all ears and it is a story definitely worth telling right here.

The ITF had taken to putting together beautiful vanity coffee table books around the Olympics. For the 2008 Beijing Games, the ITF's theme for the book was to ask players participating in the Olympics which other sport they'd love to take part in. They then asked the player for a statement as to why they picked that particular sport and set about arranging a photo shoot with the player wearing the gear from the sport they chose. Of course, some saw the photo shoot for the fun it was supposed to be. Others, as expected, whined about having to give their time to do something extra. But none of the players had any responsibility beyond showing up to have their pictures taken. Apparently, Yoni and Andy were so excited about the project they ignored the memo that all was being taken care of by the ITF as far as the photo shoot. They went about getting judo gear for themselves — the sport they picked — and arranging for the photographer to take their photos. Next thing you know, the ITF was receiving a message that the photos of Yoni and Andy were done and asking to whose attention should they be sent.

Basically, what Nick was revealing was no secret. In the best of Yiddish expressions, Yoni Erlich and Andy Ram are mensches.

By sheer luck, it turns out that Erlich and Ram — often referred to as a collective AndiYoni in Israel — both began life far away from Israel in South America.

Erlich was born on April 5, 1977 in Buenos Aires, Argentina. His family — father, Daniel, an assistant general manager of a department store, and his mother, Susana — moved to Israel when he was just 1. He started playing tennis when he was 3 when his dad took him to the local tennis courts for Saturday morning lessons.

"There was a coach throwing balls to kids who were like 3 or 4 years old — that was my start," Yoni said during a conversation at the 2013 French Open. "I was a pretty good talent, so I moved on to twice a week, three times, four times a week and then I was practicing every day. I'm the only one to play in the family. My dad wanted me to play football, basketball, tennis, everything, but I went for tennis because I was best in that."

Ram was born three years after Erlich, a fellow Aries on April 10, 1980, the son of the late Ami Ram, a professional Israeli soccer player for Beitar Jerusalem. When Ami was injured playing, he was sent to Uruguay on an outreach program where he met Ram's mother, Diana, who is a dental specialist for children. The

Andy Ram and Jonathan Erlich

family moved to Israel when Andy was 5. His inability to speak the language caused some initial issues for Andy in school so his parents took him to the tennis courts with the hope that sports would help him assimilate into his new life.

"My father used to be a sportsman, he was a professional soccer player, but he got injured when he was young in Israel," said Andy, in explaining how he came to play tennis. "So he really didn't want me to play soccer because of the injuries, so he pushed me into tennis. When I was 5, I started tennis and my parents pushed me to go every day. Growing up, I liked it and I was one of the best always in my age group — at 8, 10, 12 and it kept going."

Erlich and Ram first encountered each other at the Wingate Institute, where they both went to live and train. Despite the difficulties inherent in moving away from home early on, Ram, already determined to be a future pro, turned up at Wingate barely into his teens.

"When I was 14, I left home because I decided I wanted to be a professional," said Ram. "So I moved to the Wingate Institute near Natanya. That's where I met Jonathan. That's where I met the top athletes of Israel because they all practice there at this institute."

Despite the three-year age difference, Erlich and Ram bonded almost immediately. The duo also credit coach Ronen Moralli for helping them develop as players. Moralli originally worked in Jerusalem, but eventually moved to Wingate as a national coach. Moralli is known to have said early on of Ram that while from a technical point of view he wasn't the strongest, he was born with an uncanny understanding of the game. And any tennis player can tell you that having the innate ability to know exactly what you're supposed to be doing at every turn in a match is a skill that can only be taught to a certain level.

Initially, Yoni and Andy were pursuing singles and doubles. Then, as a duo, they reached the doubles semifinals during their second visit to Wimbledon in 2003, falling to defending champions Jonas Bjorkman and Todd Woodbridge — the Bjorkman-Woodbridge combo won the Wimbledon title from 2002 through 2004.

"The first time we had a big breakthrough was in 2003 when we made the semifinal of Wimbledon and that was kind of the breakthrough for us to stick with doubles," said Erlich, explaining why they both became dedicated to doubles. "Suddenly, we found ourselves top 50 in doubles and, by the end of the year, top 30 in the world. We decided we were very good in that, and we were young and feeling great. We had a good, opportunity to do very, very well. So we both agreed that it would be a good opportunity to have a good career. We're very happy about that choice."

While the two haven't always exclusively played with each other — at times, one or the other of them were injured — they've primarily partnered through much of their career.

In 2006, Ram made history in becoming the first Israeli to win a Grand Slam trophy. Unfortunately for Erlich, he was not along for the ride as Ram won the mixed doubles title at Wimbledon with Russian Vera Zvonareva. The following year, Ram delivered a second Grand Slam title to Israel, and again Erlich was left watching as Ram won the mixed doubles title at the 2007 French Open with Nathalie Dechy of France.

Yoni, however, would finally get his chance to be a Grand Slam champion in 2008. Along with Andy, the duo captured the Australian Open men's doubles title with a victory over the French pairing of Arnaud Clement and Michael Llodra: "Winning the Grand Slam in Australia, that was our big thing," said Erlich, smiling at the memory. "It cannot get bigger than this. It was very huge, very big at home."

In all, they have won 15 career titles together on the tour — Andy won four other titles with different partners, and Yoni won two other titles without Ram at his side. For four straight years, from 2005 to 2008, Erlich and Ram ranked Top 10 in the season-ending standings with their best year-end ranking No. 5 in 2008.

AndiYoni have also performed well in Davis Cup for Israel, leading the country to its only World Group semifinal showing in 2009. As a team, they have a 17-5 win-loss record in the international team competition. Ram has played the most Davis Cup ties in history for Israel at 26 to date: "Reaching the semifinals of Davis Cup, that was a big present for our country, just a big achievement for Israeli tennis," Erlich noted.

It was during that 2009 Davis Cup run to the semifinals, however, that Ram experienced his only real anti-Israeli moment as a pro — Erlich was at home injured. Israel was playing a first-round tie against Sweden and the weekend would take place in Malmo in early March. The city of Malmo, just a bridge crossing away from Copenhagen, Denmark, was known to have a large 30 percent Muslim population. City officials started to fear potential fan rioting in light of recent Israeli military action in Gaza. After an attempt to move the tie at the last-minute to Stockholm failed, it was decided it could be unsafe for the Israelis to allow spectators to attend the event. Indeed, there would be violent rioting on the streets as the tie was being played. So instead of having a few thousand fans rooting — a typical highlight of Davis Cup competition — there were only a few official and journalists watching the tie proceed in a cavernous arena. The ITF fined Sweden $25,000, plus extra money for the loss of gate income, and banned the country from holding Davis Cup in Malmo for at least a period of five years.

"It was shocking," Ram remembered. "The experience of playing Davis Cup without people — zero people. It wasn't anything close to what a Davis Cup feels like. It felt like practice matches with nobody there. It wasn't good for tennis and I don't think it will ever happen again."

Interestingly, that Davis Cup tie against Sweden, which Israel won 3-2, came on the heels of Israeli Shahar Pe'er being denied a visa to play at the Dubai tournament the month before all the Davis Cup controversy. After there was international outrage that Pe'er was kept out of Dubai, Ram was extended a visa to play the Dubai men's tournament.

"The following week they allowed me to go there (Dubai) and they protected me with 15 bodyguards," Andy said. "It's funny, but it was the best experience of my life because it was different. It was like I was a prime minister — I had three cars going everywhere I went and those 15 bodyguards. I remember there were like 100 reporters who wanted to talk to me. It was a funny experience, but a special experience."

As far as relationships inside the locker room, both have found that other players tend to care less about religion. Andy, who says he judges people by whether they're a "good person" spoke of playing a multi-religious doubles match in 2013 — Ram partnered with Rohan Bopanna, a Hindu, against Aisam-Ul-Haq Qureshi, a Muslim, and Jean-Julien Roger, a Catholic: "We were playing on court in Estoril. We were all from four different religions and we're all very good friends."

Neither Yoni nor Andy consider themselves particularly religious, but call themselves "traditional."

"Religion is so black and white, the rabbis and all, and that's just not us," Ram said.

While they're not regulars at attending synagogue, they adhere to keeping the fast and a reflection day of atonement for Yom Kippur, and have found tournaments are very accommodating in helping them to do so.

"We were in Bangkok and we made the final and they wanted to schedule the doubles after the singles, but that evening was the start of Yom Kippur," Erlich remembered. "We told them we wouldn't be able to play the final if the match was held after the singles, but we could play if they put it on before the singles. Luckily, the tournament director was also Jewish and following the tradition, so they listened and we played first, won the tournament, and then could celebrate."

Throughout their careers, Yoni and Andy have frequently felt the warmth and support of from fans around the world.

"When we play in the U.S., it's something really special because it's very unique," Erlich said. "In big cities, like New York and Miami, we feel the power of the Jewish tribe around the world. This is something that always warms our hearts."

CHILE'S GOLDEN BOY
Nicolas Massu

For those who encountered Nicolas Massu as a tennis player, the prevailing opinion was that here is a guy who had an edge: a hard-nosed warrior always ready to fight the good fight on court. What they didn't often see was the softer side of the Chilean, someone who worshipped his grandfather and played with passion for his country.

The fact that Nicolas Alejandro Massu even made it into this world, which he did on October 10, 1979 in Vina del Mar, Chile, is intriguing. His parents were not meant to be together — theirs would not be considered a match made in heaven. But love conquers all. So Sonia Fried, the daughter of Ladislao Fried, a Hungarian Jew who managed to escape the Nazis, and Veronika Vegvari, a survivor of the Auschwitz-Birkenau concentration camp, married Manuel Massu, who is of Palestinian Christian roots. The union of a Jew and a Palestinian raised some eyebrows, but Sonia and Manuel just ignored it all.

One only had to encounter Sonia Fried Massu to know why she got her way and married Manuel Massu. A gregarious, outgoing personality, Sonia delighted in the times when she would come to watch her son play tennis. Speaking in perfect English, Sonia openly would tell of meeting Manuel, falling in love, and in having the gumption to look beyond advice that their relationship could never work because she knew it would. Nicolas was always conscious of his unique family, and was known to comment, "I am the son of a Jewish mother and Palestinian father. Look at the weird thing that I am."

It was Massu's grandfather Ladislao, who he called Tata Laci, who introduced Nicolas to tennis when he was 5. His grandfather, who worked in real estate and the textile business, suggested his grandson abandon soccer to concentrate on tennis, and financed much of Nicolas' road through the juniors.

Massu believes that his fighting spirit — his nickname during his playing days was Vampiro — developed as a tribute to his grandfather's life. After all, how could you not admire a man who hid and ran from the Nazis and took part in resistance activities? "If my grandfather fought to survive that, why won't I be able to fight in a court to win a tennis match?" Massu told writer Leopoldo Iturra for an article for the ATP's *Deuce* publication. Interestingly, Ladislao Fried's impact extended past his family — he told his story to a production team involved in Steven Spielberg's film "Schindler's List," a story that is said to be incorporated into the movie, which grandfather and grandson watched together.

Massu was already a successful battler as a junior competitor. In 1997, Massu won the Orange Bowl singles title and then the doubles trophies at junior Wimbledon (with

Luis Horna) and the junior U.S. Open (with Fernando Gonzalez). In 1996, when still a junior, Massu was named to the Chilean Davis Cup team. He would go on to play in 28 Davis Cup ties for Chile, amassing a 32-24 total record, and was 22-12 in Davis Cup singles matches.

Massu would earn six career titles and reach nine other finals from the time he turned pro in 1997 until he formally retired from the tour in August of 2013. In 2001, he took time away from the ATP circuit to honor his heritage by playing in the Maccabiah Games.

There is no question as to the high point of Massu's career. In 2004, Nicolas became the first man in tennis history to win the Olympic gold medal in singles and doubles. There is no secret that Massu was not consid-ered the most likely to suc-ceed in Athens — that honor fell to the three top seeds: Roger Federer, Andy Roddick and Carlos Moya. But strange things tend to happen when

Nicolas Massu

you're playing for your country, and when everything was over, Massu had two golden round disks hanging around his neck. He couldn't hide his elation at winning: "I am so happy because this is my best memory in my sport career," he said in Athens. "If I look back in 10 more years, I look back on this, I'm gonna be so happy. Now I can die happy."

Massu's incredible Athens story began with winning gold in the doubles with Fernando Gonzalez. The road to their doubles victory included upsetting the top seeds Bob and Mike Bryan 7-5, 6-4 in the quarterfinals. They would defeat Nicolas Kiefer and Rainer Schuettler of Germany in the gold medal match 6-2, 4-6, 3-6, 7-6 (7), 6-4. Their victory was not only the first major title in Massu's career, but it marked the first time that Chile had ever won a gold medal at the Olympics. "It's the happiest day of my life as an athlete," he told the media after his doubles win. "To play tennis all week, to win a medal, to enter into the history of our country, I think it's a dream for anyone."

Less than 24 hours later, the 10th-seeded Massu was back on the court after beating former No. 1 Gustavo Kuerten, Vince Spadea, Igor Andreev, former No. 1 Carlos Moya, and Taylor Dent to find himself in the final against American Mardy Fish. It would take five sets for Massu to defeat the 36th-ranked Fish 6-3, 3-6, 2-6, 6-3, 6-4 to have two gold medals to pack and take home. In September of 2012, Massu told *Deuce* magazine what went through his mind during the singles final in Athens as if it took place yesterday: "In the singles final against Mardy Fish, I was extremely tired," he remembered. "I could only think, 'One point at a time.' I could only see the ball, the court and the guy in front of me. Nothing else. When I had match point, I looked up at the sky and said, 'God, please, let me win this point and I won't care about tomorrow, even if you don't want me to play tennis again in my life.' "

The latter part of Massu's career was marred by injuries — he suffered from epicondylitis — often referred to as golfer's elbow — and missed playing for a year and a half. He sustained the injury while practicing for a Davis Cup tie in Uruguay in 2012. He had a broken tendon in his left arm. Then, at 32, he was attempting to return to the tour, but despite his fight for the last point mentality, a year later, he came to the determination that a comeback would not be feasible.

On the day he retired — August 27, 2013 — at a press conference in Santiago, Chile, Massu finally showed his softer side to the world. The 33-year-old broke down in tears, placed his Olympic gold medals around his neck and hugged his mother. Retiring wasn't a decision he came to lightly — he had spent months discussing it with his team of supporters. But, in the end, he knew that he no longer could muster what it takes to be an "elite sportsman."

During the press conference to say good-bye after a 17-year career, Massu discussed how important playing for Chile had been for him. "My country can be sure that I hit each ball with all my soul and I tried to represent Chile to the fullest," Massu said. "I will miss the adrenaline of the Davis Cup, the 'chi, chi, chi' and the 'Let's go Nico' chants."

He also talked about being one of three major Chilean champions who represented their country in recent times: "With my retirement, we close two incredible decades for our sport," Massu told the crowd that included his family and most recent coach, former player Horacio de la Pena. "Marcelo Rios, Fernando Gonzalez and I contributed to put Chile's name at the top. Now we are in a transition period and others will have to lead the way to bring joy to the people with the most successful sport in Chile's history. I only pray that no comparisons arise between us, and that future generations are not given undue pressure to succeed."

And as he looked down at his Olympic medals around his neck, he probably thought back to the fact he almost lost them before he even departed Athens. So exhausted by the energy it took to win two gold medals in 24 hours, and since they played the singles final late into the night, Massu only had a few hours sleep before leaving the Olympic Village for a flight to New York and the U.S. Open. When he was getting on the plane he realized he left his gold medals next to the pillow, the very place he put them so he wouldn't forget to take them. Fortunately, Fernando Gonzalez was still in the Village and was able to retrieve the medals and deliver them to Massu in New York. Presumably, he hasn't misplaced them since.

MAGICAL MEMORIES IN MIXED COMPANY
Scott Lipsky

When Scott Lipsky was growing up in Merrick, Long Island, he dreamed about one day being a Grand Slam champion, but he believed that pursuing such a path was akin to chasing rainbows. After all, he was just a regular kid from a suburban enclave of New York City: he went to neighborhood schools, played Little League baseball and soccer, and at 13 he had his Bar Mitzvah just like many of the other boys in town.

But sometimes imaginations become reality. And for Scott Lipsky, his wish to become a Grand Slam champion came true in 2011.

It was on one of the grandest tennis stages of all time — Court Philippe Chatrier, the crown jewel of the French Open. Standing side-by-side with Australian Casey Dellacqua, the duo were unseeded and taking on the top seeds and defending champions Nenad Zimonjic of Serbia and Katarina Srebotnik of Serbia, who also won the French Open mixed title in 2006. After splitting sets, Lipsky and Dellacqua trailed 6-4 in the Super Tiebreak, but refused to fold. They went on to win six of the last seven points of the match, finally prevailing when Zimonjic pushed a backhand passing shot long.

And, just like that, Lipsky had the Grand Slam title he thought unattainable. He fell to his knees on the burnt orange dirt court and raised his arms high in triumph. The unlikely victors, Lipsky and Dellacqua put to bed a 7-6 (6), 4-6 [10-7] final victory.

"It was a lot of fun," said Lipsky, chatting during the 2014 French Open about his memories from 2011. "You know, when you go play mixed, it starts out as just fun for a little extra money, but then you get into the later rounds and it starts getting serious. Casey and I were just having fun on the court the whole time we played. It was a great experience just to get to play on Chatrier in the finals and to be able to win. To be able to say I'm a Grand Slam champion is something special. It's awesome. I didn't think it was possible I would be a Grand Slam champion, especially the mixed, no one really thinks about being a Grand Slam champion in mixed, but I'll take it any way I can get it."

Lipsky's first foray into tennis was rather unremarkable and quite a common story. He had found a racket and became mesmerized by hitting balls against the back of the house.

His family wasn't by any means a tennis family. Parents Gail and Marc were both psychologists. Marc, who passed away unexpectedly during Lipsky's freshman year at Stanford, was a runner who participated in a few marathons and triathlons. And Lipsky talks fondly of his grandfather, Jack Sherry, who, he says was a notable table tennis player around World War II time and who had played with the Shah of Iran.

But despite the lack of a tennis background, his mom and dad were happy to support their sons' self-driven interest in tennis. So when young Scott asked for tennis lessons they obliged. Lipsky would spend from age six to 13 playing at the Port Washington Tennis Academy, a facility that also counted the likes of John McEnroe, the late Vitas Gerulaitis and Mary Carillo among the many former stars who learned the game on its courts. By the time he was 11 or 12, he also started at Robbie Wagner's Tournament Training Center in Glen Cove and stayed with that program throughout high school.

Lipsky might've been a highly-ranked player nationally, but it didn't prevent him from playing on his high school tennis team. After all, he liked being just like the other kids.

And when he arrived to play on the team, he didn't try to push his star quality on coach Alan Fleishman, who was informed by the other players on the team that the

Scott Lipsky

new freshman kid should be their lead player. In an article that Fleishman, who has remained a close friend to Lipsky, penned in *Long Island Tennis Magazine* on June 3, 2011, he wrote of the first time he laid his eyes on Lipsky: "Fifteen years ago I was a high school coach at John F. Kennedy High School in Bellmore, N.Y. One day, a player came out and, like Moses at the Red Sea, 'parted the waters.' 'Put him on the first court,' the kids said. 'Why? He's a freshman,' I said. 'He's ranked nationally and internationally,' the kids shot back."

"I went to actual school all the way through," said Lipsky, who lost only one match during his entire high school career. "It was great for me. I think if I had gone to an academy I would've burnt out. It was great for me to go to normal school. They were great letting me travel and miss days and weeks, but it was definitely better for me."

Away from high school, Lipsky played junior tennis against some very good players, chief among them Andy Roddick and Mardy Fish. Assessing his own abilities in relation to Roddick and Fish, Lipsky had little trouble determining he should go to college and was thrilled when Stanford came calling.

"I wasn't ready to play professionally when I was 18, and my parents didn't want me to go professional, they wanted me to go get a college degree," said Lipsky, who graduated Stanford in 2003 with a major in American Studies. "You know, it's really hard to make it in tennis and to have an opportunity to play at a school like Stanford where you have the best tennis and it's also a great academic school — it was kind of a no-brainer."

A three-time All-American at Stanford, Lipsky played on the Cardinal squad that won the 2000 NCAA Team Championship. During college, he bonded with fellow Cardinal David Martin, who became his close friend and constant doubles partner. So it came as little surprise that, diplomas in hand, the two buddies set out together to attempt to make a living playing professional tennis.

"When I graduated in '03 I played singles and doubles at the Futures and Challengers until the end of 2006, so, for two and a half to three years," Lipsky recounted. "And my doubles rankings were always higher and I was always doing better in doubles. My singles ranking got up to about 315 and my doubles ranking was about 100 at the end of 2006. I just kind of decided I didn't want to play Futures and Challengers anymore. I wanted to go play ATP-level tournaments, so my doubles partner and I — David Martin and I — we decided we were going to start just playing doubles. In 2007, we got a wild card into San Jose and made the semifinals. And then we qualified at Wimbledon and made the third round there. From that point on, we were into ATP tournaments every week. It's been great. To get to play tournaments at the highest level against the top players in the game is definitely worth it."

Martin stopped playing after the 2011 season and Lipsky has soldiered on with other partners, winning 11 doubles titles by the end of 2013.

In 2010, with Martin at his side as his best man, Lipsky married former Olympian Marie Mijalis, a kayaker. Their son, Matthew, was born in 2013. Marie works full-time for Pfizer pharmaceuticals, which prevents the family from traveling with Scott during much of the year.

And as for his Jewish background, Lipsky admitted he's not from a religious family and his involvement in the religion has waned even more as an adult.

"Not too strong at this point," said Lipsky, when asked about his Jewish identity. "When I was younger, yeah, my parents were Jewish and we went to the temple once in awhile and I was Bar Mitvah'ed. But I kind of fell out of it a little bit."

FROM WAR HERO TO WORLD NO. 1
Noam Gershony

There aren't many players who can start playing tennis at age 27 and only a few years later become the No. 1 player in the world, but that's how it happened for Israeli Noam Gershony. In fact, Gershony is the only Jewish player since the advent of computer rankings in the sport to attain the highest ranking achievable.

By now, readers are likely scratching their heads trying to figure out how Noam Gershony escaped their notice, or have determined I have no idea what I'm talking about. Well, let me introduce everyone to Noam — an Apache helicopter pilot, a genuine war hero and a world champion. Yes, at the 2012 Paralympic Games in London, Gershony won the gold medal in the men's singles quad competition and the bronze medal in doubles.

"It's funny because only after the London Paralympics I was ranked No. 1 in the world," Gershony said. "I could have never imagined such a thing and it was a great feeling and a great honor."

Noam Gershony was born in Israel on January 30, 1983, a perfectly able-bodied individual. And like many youngsters, Noam loved participating in sports, but in no way was destined for a career as a professional tennis player: "I used to take some tennis lessons before (my) injury and I played with my friends, but not competitively," he said. "I played soccer, basketball and volleyball as well."

When Gershony grew up, he went off to serve in the military, as all Israelis do. He became an elite Apache helicopter pilot with the Israeli Defense Force (IDF).

It was during the second Lebanon War in 2006 that Noam nearly gave his life for his country. Along with copilot Ran Yehoshua Kochva, Noam was heading to the Lebanese border where their assignment was to assist Israeli troops on the ground in the combat zone. They never made it to their destination. An in-air collision with another IDF helicopter near Ramot Naftali caused Gershony's helicopter to crash. Yehoshua Kochva didn't survive the crash, but when the IDF's search and rescue unit arrived, they found Noam still alive, barely. He had serious wounds, lost a lot of blood, and suffered multiple fractures — the medical personnel on the scene thought he had little to no chance to survive. Although the prevailing opinion was that there was not much hope for Gershony, he was airlifted to Rambam Medical Center in Haifa. That airlift journey was harrowing — the helicopter carrying Noam had to make two emergency stops along the route, one after a respiratory collapse and a second in an open field when his blood pressure bottomed out at zero.

After experiencing the nightmare every parent with a child in military service dreads — the knock on the door to tell them that their child is injured, or even worse had died in battle — the Gershonys were offered little encouragement by doctors. "They took us to the hospital and said the situation with Noam was critical," his father, Moshe, told Israeli news media. A week later, however, doctors were able to pronounce that Gershony would live.

Life, however, would be very different for Noam. He was now disabled and would have to go through operations and a long period of rehabilitation therapy. But as Noam had already proven during this fight for survival, he was resolute in continuing to live life as he always had — to its fullest extent possible.

Noam Gershony

"It was a miracle that I was saved," Gershony said to *Ynet*, the online news service. "From the moment that I got my life back as a gift, I promised myself that I wouldn't waste it."

A physiotherapist suggested that wheelchair tennis would be an ideal activity during his recovery, so he took up the sport: "I think playing sports is the best way to rehabilitate," Gershony told me about how tennis helped his rehabilitation. "It's very important to move your body and to be active as fast as you can after getting out of the hospital. Playing sports is good for the soul. Tennis was the first sport I've tried after the injury and I enjoyed it a lot."

By 2010, he was playing on the elite ITF wheelchair circuit that tours the world. I watched Noam play at the now-defunct Florida Open held at Patch Reef Park in Boca Raton, Fla. in April 2011. It was his second year playing on the international circuit and as an unseeded entry in the draw, he made quite the splash during the week. He upset David Wagner of the U.S., the No. 1 player in the world. He ended up losing to No. 2 Peter Norfolk of Britain in the final. At the time, Norfolk accurately predicted a bright future in the game for Gershony: "It's exciting that we have some new players coming up in the quad division," Norfolk said. "Gershony is a player to watch."

Gershony's moment in time came in 2012 — he captured the French Open quad title to become the No. 2 ranked player in the world. And later that summer, he won the gold medal at the London Paralympics to achieve the world No. 1 ranking.

* * * *

If it wasn't for Ludwig Guttman, a German Jew who emigrated to the United Kingdom to escape the Nazis, neither Noam Gershony nor any of the other Paralympians would have had a forum to showcase their amazing athletic prowess.

After volunteering as an orderly in an Accident Hospital for Coalminers in 1917 and seeing patients with spinal injuries die relatively quickly, Guttman followed a path into medicine. He became a neurosurgeon specializing in patients with spinal injuries. Once in Britain, Guttman was asked to open a spinal unit at Stoke Mandeville hospital. His work helped to keep patients with spinal injuries alive as he took note that urinary tract infections and sepsis from bed sores were two chief causes for these patients dying unnecessarily. He also understood that those with spinal cord injuries needed a mental boost and a reason to live.

In 1948, when the Olympics were held in London, Guttman brought sports to his patients in Stoke Mandeville, rounding up 16 patients for a first-ever archery competition, which he kept going every year. In 1952, he invited a few Dutch patients to take part in his archery event, which gave the tournament an international flavor. But even that wasn't widespread enough for Guttman, who pushed for even more. In 1960, 400 athletes from 23 countries arrived in Rome just like the able-bodied Olympians, for what became the first Olympics for disabled athletes, although they wouldn't officially be called the Paralympics until 1988.

Guttman's fame came back into the picture when the Olympics and Paralympics returned to London in 2012 — the games where Gershony won his gold medal and where other international Paralympic athletes gathered to compete. At the London Jewish Museum, they timed an exhibit about Guttman, who was knighted by the Queen in 1966, around the Olympics and Paralympics. The BBC ran a documentary called "The Best of Men" highlighting Guttman, the father of the Paralympics. A bust of Guttman, who passed away in 1980, debuted at the 2012 Games and will appear at all future Paralympic sites.

In an article penned by Miriam Shaviv in *The Times of Israel* on August 27, 2012, the chief executive of London's Jewish Museum, Abigail Morris, said of Guttman, "Hitler tried to kill all the Jews and people with disabilities. Thanks to his actions, Guttman ended up here in the UK, and this year over 4,000 athletes will compete in London at the Paralympic Games. It's the triumph of human spirit over adversity."

* * * *

While no one knew how Noam would fare at the London Paralympics — that's why they play the matches, games and tournaments in sports — a group of Noam's friends were confident he'd go the distance before the Paralympics started. His buddies from the Air Force wanted to be in London to root for Noam, so they purchased tickets, but only for the semifinals and finals.

His friends, who sat in the stand wearing white T-shirts that they adorned with hand-drawn Israeli flags on the front, watched and cheered as Gershony bypassed American David Wagner 6-3, 6-1 in the Quad Wheelchair gold medal match. Gershony, the former helicopter pilot, had become Israel's first Paralympic gold medalist since 2004. Prior to winning the quad singles, Gershony had already picked up bronze with Shraga Weinberg in the doubles. His success was rewarded when fellow Paralympians selected Noam to carry the Israeli flag in the closing ceremonies.

But his most cherished moment came when the gold medal was draped around his neck and the Israeli national anthem Hatikvah played as the Israeli flag was raised. His parents, his coach Nimrod Bichler, who cried in the stands, and his friends and fans were all there to share the moment with him. And what they observed was a 29-year-old former soldier, who came close to giving his life for his country, become overwhelmed to the point of shedding tears of joy: "The fact that they were all there made it extra special," Noam said. "They were there for me every day at the Rehab Center and shared some difficult times with me. I can't even begin to describe what it feels like to win the gold medal — such a powerful and breathtaking experience."

I asked Noam to remember back to what was going through his mind at the time of the award ceremony to which he said: "I was injured in a war, serving my country, my people, the Israel flag and the Jewish nation brought up all the emotions. I was so proud to see the Israeli flag and to hear Hatikvah, which always moves me whenever I hear it."

In case anyone is of the opinion that Noam's accomplishment went by unnoticed, think again. In Israel, it was huge news.

Fellow player Shahar Pe'er took note, saying, "I want to commend Noam on his amazing achievement. To top the world's best players at the Paralympic Games is an unbelievable success. You've inspired all of us."

Gershony had a relationship with the other Israeli players, saying, "They were always great supporters and were always joking they'll never beat me playing in a chair. So I always say, 'Don't feel bad, I'll never beat you standing on my legs.' "

Beyond Pe'er, there was a strong showing of Israeli dignitaries taking the time to express their pride in Gershony's success.

Benny Gantz, the Israel Defense Force Chief of Staff weighed in, stating, "I salute you on behalf of IDF on your exceptional determination and achievements." Gantz also invited Gershony to visit with him when he came home to Israel.

Israeli President Shimon Perez, who phoned Gershony, released this congratulatory message for the gold medalist: "You proved that you are as good on court as you are in the sky, talented in the Apache and tennis. We are very proud of you. This is the best news we could have received this weekend."

And Prime Minister Benjamin Netanyahu, who also called Noam, said of the golden hero of Israel: "I was very emotional when I saw you win. The state of Israel embraces you on this great achievement. You symbolize the triumph of the human spirit over the difficulties of life."

For Gershony, hearing from the most important Israelis was something he'll never forget. "It was a great privilege and a great honor," Noam said. "The leaders of my country all came to share their respect and support for the Paralympic team. It also helped bringing the disabled sports to the headlines of the news and that can help other people with disabilities go out and try to do things themselves and gain more confident in their abilities."

As if winning the gold and bronze medals and being lauded by the most famous Israelis wasn't enough for this shy, unassuming athlete, Gershony was selected by the readers of *The Jerusalem Post* as the 2012 Israeli Sports Personality of the Year. While he thanked those who voted for him, he also had this humble message for his legion of fans: "It is slightly embarrassing because I don't think that I deserve to be the sports personality of the year. There are people who underwent a much more significant process and deserve far more recognition than I do. I was lucky that I won the gold medal, but there were amazing athletes in the Olympic and Paralympic delegations that I was honored just to be on the same team with. So to receive this is beyond an honor because I feel there are others who deserve it more."

OPENING CLOSED DOORS: STANDING UP FOR WHAT'S RIGHT

Shahar Pe'er

When I wrote a story for ESPN.com after a long sit-down with Shahar Pe'er at the February 2012 Qatar Total Open in Doha, I started the article with the following lead: "Just like any other tennis player who competes on the international WTA tour, Shahar Pe'er is a citizen of the world. But unlike any of the other top 100 players, the 24-year-old is also a citizen of Israel, and on occasion that has delivered complications in her career."

For some, traveling the world as an athlete from Israel, a country that is beloved by many and despised by others, could be too demanding and difficult a role to handle. But not for Shahar Pe'er — she's happy to be the person to open doors that have been previously closed: "I think in sports, if we can break down barriers, it's very important," Shahar told me while we chatted a year later at the 2013 French Open. "We don't want it to be all about politics, but with sports sometimes it's perfect for you to do that."

Indeed, Pe'er made headlines around the world in 2009, although that was not her intention. Pe'er was playing the Pattaya City tournament in Thailand and was heading from there to the next tour stop in Dubai in the United Arab Emirates, or so she thought. Although Israel and the UAE share no diplomatic relations — the UAE does not recognize the existence of Israel — Pe'er never anticipated there would be a problem. She had direct entry into the event and had a positive prior experience in an Arab country the year before, so she put the tournament on her schedule.

In 2008, the 17th-ranked Pe'er entered — and played — at the Doha, Qatar tournament without incident, becoming the first Israeli female tennis player to compete in a Persian Gulf country. She traveled with her older brother, Shlomi, as well as a coach, and reached the third round. At the time of her 2008 visit, the Doha tournament director Ayman Azmy was quoted as saying, "Naturally, it is clear evidence that all nations are welcome in Doha to participate in our event." Pe'er believed her first trip to Doha went well: "I have been received with a lot of warmth by people in Doha. I have been made to feel welcome by everybody I have come across so far."

Unfortunately, prior experience did not turn out to be an accurate benchmark for Pe'er to be welcomed in Dubai. She was only two hours from boarding her flight to Dubai when she was told she wouldn't be granted a visa to enter the country. Tournament organizers were concerned that fans would protest a recent military offensive in Gaza if Pe'er showed up in Dubai.

When word started to trickle out that Sha'har Pe'er had been denied entry to play in Dubai, there was a major outcry heard around the globe. Fellow player Andy Roddick withdrew from the men's Dubai event the following week in protest, releasing the statement, "I really didn't agree with what went on over there." The Tennis Channel was supposed to televise the event but Ken Solomon, their CEO and Chairman of the Board, who also happens to be Jewish, pulled the plug on their coverage. *The Wall Street Journal* cut their sponsorship to the event. And when Venus Williams won the tournament, she took the opportunity at the award ceremony to declare Pe'er was wronged by being denied a visa.

Larry Scott, who headed the WTA at the time — and yes, happens to be Jewish — had given some thought to canceling the tournament on the spot, but after a conversation with Shahar allowed the event to go on. The WTA, however, not only fined the Dubai tournament a record $300,000, but Scott made it very clear to event organizers if the situation wasn't rectified for the future, the tournament would lose its tour sanction. And just one week later the Dubai event, obviously realizing the situation needed to be rectified, granted Israeli doubles player Andy Ram a visa to play in the men's tournament.

Fast forward one year to February of 2010, and this time, Shahar boarded the plane to Dubai knowing she'd be granted a visa. While she was en route, Shahar was fine, but admits she felt some trepidation upon landing in Dubai. Her nerves calmed down once she saw her dad, Dovik, a former computer software specialist, waiting for her at the airport.

Besides being part of a historic moment, Shahar had already seen that the Dubai draw had not been kind to her.

All she could hope for was that she didn't fight the good fight to be able to play in Dubai just to lose in the first round.

Beyond that, there was an unexpected political aspect that inconveniently arose in the last few weeks before her visit. Whether it's fair or not, when it comes to Israel and the neighboring Arab countries, the citizens are caught up in a conflict that dates to ancient times. Within the month before Shahar journeyed to the UAE, Mahmoud al-Mabhouh, a top-level Palestinian Hamas commander was killed in Dubai. The prevailing opinion in the UAE is that Israelis entered the country with British passports and were responsible for al-Mabhouh's assassination. In an effort to keep Shahar safe and secure while at the tournament, she was kept within a limited area and had a large security detail wherever she went.

"At the beginning, I was a bit worried and I didn't know how to feel and I got a lot, a lot, a lot of security," she said. "I was very separated from the rest of the players so I hadn't seen anyone. I had my own court to play on so that was very different. I felt the tournament — the people were really taking care of me."

Why did she even want to play in Dubai? The answer was simple: "My ranking was good enough to get in and it was a $2-million tournament — one of the biggest," she said to me four years later. "So it's not fair that other players can play and I cannot play. I mean, if I hadn't had the ranking it's a different story. I think I deserved the same equal opportunity like the other players."

Surprisingly, Shahar actually thrived under the unusual circumstances of her first visit to Dubai. She was right that

her draw had many poten-
tial pitfalls but she survived
through to the semifinals. She
defeated 14th-ranked Yanina
Wickmayer, Virginie Razzano,
top seed Caroline Wozniacki
and Li Na before falling to
Venus Williams. After she
beat Wickmayer in three sets,
the emotion of the moment
got to her and she started to
cry in relief of winning the

Sharar Peer

match. Pe'er was not the only one inspired by her incredible
performance at that 2010 Dubai tournament — Venus
Williams was most impressed with Pe'er's courage and ability to compete under such scrutiny: "I can't imagine playing
as well as Shahar in these circumstances," Williams said at
the time. "I have to give her congratulations and props. She's
courageous. I don't think anyone else on tour could do what
she's doing."

Shahar Pe'er is a Sabra, a daughter of Israel born in
Jerusalem on May 1, 1987. Pe'er's mother, Aliza, is a child
of Czechoslovakian Jews who were Holocaust survivors
from the Slovakian part of the country. Shahar's paternal
grandmother was an Israeli nurse and her grandfather was a
South African doctor. Her dad spent his first six years living
in South Africa, but when his father passed away, the family
moved back to Israel.

The Pe'er family fits the profile of a secular Jewish family who celebrate the holidays and enjoy having Friday night

Sabbath dinner: "I'm not religious in things, like I don't eat Kosher, we're not Kosher in the house. I drive on Saturday. But we do make a Kiddush on Friday night and we do keep Yom Kippur and Passover. You know, the tradition things we do, but nothing more than that. It's nice — as a family we always had dinner together every night, but we always liked Friday night as special and we'd wait for that with the Kiddush."

Shahar came to tennis as many players do, by following her older siblings — sister Shani and brother Shlomi — to the sport. Shahar would accompany her mother when she would drive Shani and Shlomi to the courts every day and one day her sister's coach said he saw something in Shahar's eyes that made him think she'd be good at the game. Who knows what it was he saw in her eyes, if anything, but Shahar definitely took to the sport: "I was very good from the beginning, from the first time I started to play," she said.

By the time Shahar was 12, she had won her first international junior title, teaming with Nicole Vaidisova of the Czech Republic to win the Eddie Herr doubles trophy. She also reached the singles final at the event.

In 2001, Shahar won the Orange Bowl 14-and-under singles title in Miami. And, in 2004, she won the Australian Open junior girls' trophy by beating Nicole Vaidisova in the final. She was the first Israeli girl to win a junior Grand Slam title since Anna Smashnova won the 1990 French Open junior girls' competition.

Israel is a country that has mandatory military service for all citizens. For Shahar, her time in the army commenced in November 2005, which coincided with her early days on the tour. She spent 10 days doing basic training — she excelled at rifle marksmanship — and then served around her travel schedule. When in Israel, she'd spend a few hours a day working in a military office primarily doing secretarial work: "Basic training was easy for me," she said. "You know, as a tennis player, I'm used to having order in my day, to wake up early and practice."

Since Pe'er joined the pro tour in the mid-2000s she has had mixed results. At times, she played like she was on the verge of Top 10, which she was in January of 2011 when she attained a career high ranking of No. 11. In 2007, she became the first Israeli woman to reach a Grand Slam quarterfinal, doing so at the Australian Open and U.S. Open. At other times, however, she has struggled to find her form — she ended the 2012 and '13 seasons ranked in the 70s.

When we spoke at the 2013 French Open, Shahar was in a period when her game was not at its best. In fact, when the French Open concluded, countrywoman Julia Glushko had trumped Pe'er as the top-ranked Israeli woman. By the end of July, 2013, order had been restored and Shahar was back in position as the top Israeli woman player. But she's happy to know that Glushko, who emigrated to Israel from the Ukraine with her teaching pro parents when she was 9, is right there with her representing Israel.

And as she has matured, she is seeing things a little bit differently: "I've developed a lot in the last half a year as a person and it's really important for me to keep developing," Pe'er said. "I'm not the same person as I was a few years ago. I realize I'm a tennis player and I have to work for this — if it's my job it's my job. As a little girl I only cared about tennis.

Now I have more things I'm interested in — family, friends, life, to have a boyfriend. I'm a person first and tennis is my job, but tennis is not who I am."

One of her outside interests is being a foodie, a good choice when you get to travel the world to experience different types of food and the best of restaurants. She also likes to cook, primarily desserts and pastries, although you couldn't tell by her figure.

What has remained a constant for Shahar is her attempt to spend the most important holidays at home with her family. But the WTA calendar doesn't always cooperate with when the holidays fall. She's willing to play matches on Rosh Hashanah, the Jewish New Year, but will not play on Yom Kippur — the men's and women's tour respect the request from any Jewish player unwilling to play on the Day of Atonement.

Pe'er is also very dedicated to commemorating Yom HaShoah — Holocaust Remembrance Day — which comes every year a week after Passover. When she has played on that day, as she did on April 8, 2013 at the Katowice, Poland tournament, she wore a black armband with the words Never Again written on it. On her Facebook page that day, she offered the following post from Katowice, which is less than an hour's drive from Auschwitz: "I am in Poland, which makes the upcoming Yom HaShoah all the more real. My heart goes out to all the innocent people who lost their lives during the Holocaust. Never Again."

In 2010, the same year when she first played in Dubai, Shahar was asked to lead that year's "March of the Living" from Auschwitz to the Birkenau concentration camp. She immediately agreed to the honor and her mom quickly said she wanted to walk too. Mother and daughter then extended an invitation to her grandma, Yuliana Eckstein, to join them for the walk. At first, her 82-year-old grandmother was reluctant to make a first trip back to Auschwitz since she was there during the war. The memories of suffering through the cold and snow in a skimpy dress, and eating a small piece of bread every once in a while, might become too real if she returned. Eckstein had never spoken to her family about the ordeal she lived through until Shahar's sister, Shani, asked about it for a school assignment. At the last minute, only a week away from the walk, Shahar's grandmother decided she should make the trip to walk alongside her daughter and granddaughter.

"It was amazing," Shahar remembered. "We were three generations from one family and I was leading the "March of the Living." My grandma, she was there in Auschwitz when she was small so it was tough for her to come back, really difficult because it was part of her life. It was a very tough moment, but, for me, it was also such a great pride."

MIXED ALLEGIANCES NORTH AND SOUTH OF THE BORDER
Jesse Levine

Like many of the other Jewish players who have competed at the upper echelon of tennis, Jesse Levine has a strong sense of what it means to be culturally Jewish.

Where Levine tends to deviate from the other members of the tribe who've played the game is he considers himself a practicing Jew from the religious perspective. It's the way Jesse, a dual Canadian-American citizen, was brought up and it remains a strong priority in his life.

Levine was born in Ottawa, Canada, to a Canadian mother, Brenda, and American father, Nathan, who hails from State College, Pennsylvania, the home of Penn State, where he played college tennis. Jesse grew up in the Centrepointe community of Ottawa, where there was a heavy emphasis on his being Jewish, including his attending a Jewish Day School.

"My mom's side of the family in Ottawa is more religious than my dad's side," said Levine, chatting at Wimbledon eight years from when he became a Grand Slam champion by winning the 2005 Wimbledon junior boys' doubles title with Michael Shabazz. "Obviously, my dad's family is Jewish and brought him up Jewish. I remember when I was in seventh or eighth grade, I had a Bar or Bat Mitzvah to go to every single weekend when I lived in Canada because I went to Hebrew Day School. It wasn't a Yeshiva — it was called Hillel Academy — it was casual and we learned English, French and Hebrew in the same day and then I'd go and do sports after school."

As his time on the 13-year-old Bar-and-Bat Mitzvah party circuit was coming to a close, so was Jesse's life in Canada. The family was about to embark on a new adventure in the United States, moving to Boca Raton, Florida, for a number of reasons. First, Jesse's three years younger brother, Daniel, had suffered

Jesse Levine

from ulcerative colitis since he was 8 and the family was told the Florida climate could be an elixir for the disease. Second, his father, a commercial property insurance broker, had an exciting job opportunity. And for Jesse, the year-round sunny weather would be a bonus for his pursuit of tennis.

Once in Florida, Levine enrolled at Boca Prep, a nondenominational preparatory school across the street from the Evert Tennis Academy where he trained. He then moved across the state to the Nick Bollettieri Academy for his last two years of high school.

Throughout his youth, Jesse, who would top the growth charts at 5 feet 9 and the scales at around 150 pounds, participated in a variety of sports, including soccer, baseball, basketball and tennis. But in his teens, he came to the conclusion that if his life was going to be sports, he'd have to make a choice. And that choice ended up being an easy one to make.

"My dad played college tennis at Penn State, so he kind of got me into the sport and I just loved it at a young age," Levine said. "I actually played all sports growing up in Ottawa — I played soccer, baseball, basketball and tennis, all in different leagues, but tennis was definitely my best sport. And once I reached about 15, 16, I realized that was the only sport that I really had a chance to go to a Division I school on (a college) scholarship. Soccer, I got offers from smaller D-II and D-III schools, but I didn't want to do that. I was too short for basketball and not quite good enough for baseball. I was OK at soccer but not nearly as good as I was in tennis, so I decided to focus on one sport."

And indeed, Levine did go off to the University of Florida, a Division I college, where he played for the Gators for one season. But tour life was calling and Jesse answered.

A talented left-hander, Levine is a grinder on the court. With his height and weight class, his strengths are speedy court coverage and an attitude that bolsters the theory there's always one more ball to hit unless your opponent makes a mistake. Levine received quite a lot of help from the United States Tennis Association's Player Development program and ranked as high as No. 69 in singles in October 2012.

In 2009, he partnered with fellow Gator Ryan Sweeting to reach the Houston doubles final.

Levine's terrier-like quality on a court attracted the attention of Roger Federer, who determined that Jesse would be an ideal training partner. In 2007, Levine joined Federer for a number of practice weeks in Dubai, UAE, where the Swiss maestro maintains a home. Levine admits he had some initial trepidation about traveling to the Arab country.

"My family brought me up to be proud to be Jewish," Levine said. "I wear a Mezuzah around my neck at all times. The only time I was a little bit nervous wearing it was when I went to Dubai, but I honestly had no problem."

For the most part, the affable Levine is a player who primarily stays under the radar. Nevertheless, at the end of 2012 he became something of a headline story. After years of playing tennis as an American, Jesse decided it was time to represent Canada. So, in early 2013, instead of playing for the stars-and-stripes, Levine delineated his country affiliation by a maple leaf.

As a courtesy, Levine kept his decision to switch allegiances under wraps until he had an opportunity to explain his plans to the USTA's Player Development head honcho, Patrick McEnroe, and coach, Jay Berger. Following the move, Levine would joke that the American players had taken to calling him by a new nickname: "Air Canada."

One thing that is definitely not destined to change is his dedication to a Jewish way of life. As a child, he would attend the Ottawa synagogue where his uncle was the President every Saturday. Nowadays, with all the travel, synagogue is more reserved for the holidays, but he's been known to take in Saturday services at the Boca Raton Chabad near his home. While his attempts to keep Kosher on the road ran into continual roadblocks, when he's home he always sticks to the traditional dietary laws.

And, not surprisingly, when it's time for Jesse to consider marriage, the family's expectations are he will remember his roots.

"Obviously, my mom and my dad want me to marry somebody who, by their books, is Jewish, obviously with the mom being Jewish," said Levine, referring to the belief of who is and isn't Jewish. "I know my Zaide (grandfather) back in Canada says if we're going to marry a non-Jew they have to be converted by a certain rabbi. My family sticks to the guidelines."

And then he adds a final codicil. "Obviously, they just want me to be happy, but they'd be happy if I marry Jewish," he said, laughing.

GUSHING OVER ISRAEL
Julia Glushko

Being Jewish in Ukraine came with its limitations. So it was no wonder that Julia Glushko's paternal grandfather dreamed of relocating, of making a reality of the common phrase, "Next year in Jerusalem."

Unfortunately, her grandfather passed away before he realized his hopes of becoming an Israeli. But in 1999, a few years after his death, Glushko's family fulfilled her grandfather's wish and left their Ukrainian home in Donetsk for a brighter future in Israel.

There were a number of rationalizations why Glushko's parents, Sergey and Olga, both teaching pros, decided it was in their best interest to leave Ukraine behind. One obvious motivating factor for the family immigrating to Israel was a prevalent sentiment of anti-Semitism in their homeland: "I don't remember it, but my parents do," said Julia, while playing at the 2013 French Open. "That was one of the reasons why we moved."

But it wasn't the only purpose behind Julia's parents pulling up stakes. They wanted Julia and her brother, Alex, who went on to serve in Special Forces in the Israeli army, to have a better life. For the children, the move was easy but Julia knew it was a difficult and selfless decision for her parents.

"We moved in 1999," Glushko remembered. "It was different. It was exciting and I was little, only 9 years old. It was harder for my parents because they moved to nothing. They didn't have friends or family there. They just decided to move because we are Jewish and they thought that me and my brother would have way more opportunities than in the Ukraine and I think that it's true."

The family initially settled in Jerusalem, but eventually relocated to Ramat HaSharon near Tel Aviv, where the Israel Tennis Center's first facility is located. For Glushko, it's hard to remember a time when she didn't have a tennis racket in hand and was spending time on the tennis court. But she does know that she began pursuing the sport more seriously when she was 6 years old.

As a child, Glushko idolized Serena Williams and Martina Hingis and would get to know both when she spent some time training at the Patrick Mouratoglou Tennis Academy outside of Paris. Her younger sister, Lina, a Sabra born a year and a half after the family moved to Israel, was thrilled to take a photo with Serena when she came to watch Julia play at the French Open in 2013.

As Glushko got older, her parents backed away from coaching her, leaving that responsibility to others such as Liran Kling and Assaf Ingber. It was everyone's belief that it would be better to keep family about family and not tennis.

A player who relies on power shots from the baseline and fluid movements around the court, Glushko's first objective was to rank in the top 100. She realized that goal in 2013, ending the year ranked No. 91. Her next goal is to join those players ranked among the top 50.

One ambition Glushko claims she never had was to replace the three years older Shahar Pe'er as Israel's No. 1 women's player. An intention or not, Glushko became Israel's top female player for the first time in the June 6, 2013 rankings — Julia was ranked No. 131 and Shahar was No. 171.

Julia Glushko

"I think it's nice, but we don't have many players so I'd prefer me and Shahar go up together," said Glushko, who had won eight singles and eight doubles ITF-level titles by June 2014. "There are a lot of players in the world still ranked ahead of me. So I'm not concentrating on being No. 1 in Israel, especially when it's Shahar dropping. I've known Shahar since a very young age. We often travel together and we're on the same Fed Cup team for six years now. We're good friends."

Glushko finds that one of the biggest benefits of her life as a professional tennis player is the opportunity to travel. She loves to see and experience different places in the world, although she admits there are some locales where she prefers to keep her Israeli nationality under wraps.

"I love traveling — I love new places," Glushko said. "I love New York; it's probably one of my favorite cities, and it's my dream to live there for a year or two one day just to experience it. I love Vancouver; it's one of the most beautiful places. I love Auckland; it's very pretty. And I really like Buenos Aires. But I guess Tel Aviv is my favorite — it's home and it has everything. All kind of people, the nice beach, the food, the atmosphere is just amazing."

For Julia, Judaism is more about the culture of the religion rather than the practice of religion. While she requests not to play on Yom Kippur just like most of the Jewish players, she isn't someone to closely follow Jewish doctrine.

"I love the holidays — Pesach, Hanukkah — it's really nice because it brings the family together so I like the tradition," she said. "I'm not religious at all. I think that in life it's the most important that you're a good person and not that you eat or don't eat pork. Some people do it and I respect it. One of my best friends, she's not real religious, but she keeps Kosher and her mom doesn't drive on Shabbat. But for me, personally, it's not that important."

Glushko might not choose to live life to the letter of the Jewish law. But the fact that she is Jewish — and an Israeli — is never far from her thoughts. And both make her feel exceptionally lucky and proud.

"I think being Jewish is very special," said Glushko, emphatically. "I feel like I'm an Israeli tennis player. You know, in Israel, people are very patriotic. Like some people around the world don't play for their country, like in Fed Cup. In Israel, it's impossible. You can't not play and I love it, it's one of the most amazing experiences to play for your country, and when you have Israel written on your back, everyone is supporting you and it's an amazing feeling."

OTHER JEWISH QUALIFIERS

The story of the Jewish players told in this book is by no means the story of all the Jewish players who've ever played the game of tennis at the highest level. Indeed, there are many other players who would be eligible to be included in these pages. Here are some of the other Jewish players listed in alphabetical order: Ivan Baron, Noam Behr, Gilad Bloom, Audra Cohen, Stephanie Cohen Aloro, Gaston Etlis, Sharon Fichman, Zach Fleishman, Eric Fromm, Dana Gilbert, Camila Giorgi, Drew Gitlin, Paul Goldstein, Seymour Greenberg, Jimmy Gurfein, Amir Hadad, Harold Hecht, Anita Kanter, Steve Krulevitz, Andrea Leand, Harel Levy, Bruce Manson, Ricky Meyer, Stacy Margolin, Steve Meister, Ricky Meyer, Tzipora Obziler, Wayne Odesnik, Noam Okun, Shahar Perkiss, Eyal Ran, Sergio Roitman, Jeff Salzenstein, Howard Schoenfield, David Schneider, Dudi Sela, Andrew Sznajder, Amir Weintraub and Robbie Weiss.

We encourage readers to share any stories or comments with us on our Facebook page and on Twitter at @ JewishTennis

Vic Seixas Note

Some readers will be wondering why Vic Seixas hasn't been included in the book. The simple answer is that Seixas has through the years been quite emphatic that he is not Jewish. It is true that the family name Seixas has a strong history in Sephardic Judaism, including in his native city of Philadelphia. There are some that insist they remember Seixas' parents being Jewish. However, it is known that Seixas isn't exclusively a Jewish name and as much as Jewish tennis fans might want to claim the former Wimbledon and U.S. champion, it's hard to disrespect Seixas' own resolve that he isn't a Jew.

Helen Jacobs Note

There are many who believe that Helen Jacobs, a five-time major singles champion, was Jewish. It is felt that at the very least through her father, Ronald H. Jacobs, she would be. She was known to identify herself as a Christian, so she is not included in the book.

JEWISH CONNECTIONS

Boris Becker

Boris Becker, the German wunderkind who conquered Wimbledon for the first time as an athletic and daring 17-year-old, would be a player who many would least likely expect to have a Jewish background.

But, alas, it is true and we know it because back in his youth Boris was the one to bring up his Jewish heritage. He spoke about his mother, the former Elvira Pisch, having to flee her native Czechoslovakia when the Russians invaded. He then spoke of her Jewish heritage, later on making note that she was raised a Catholic — she certainly wouldn't be the first Jewish person during the World War II era to be raised in another faith in an effort to escape the Nazi fate.

One of the occasions in which Becker addressed his having a Jewish background was in an interview with Bill Simons, the Publisher and Editor of *Inside Tennis*. Becker told Simons in an interview around 1999-2000 the following: "If you just look at my background, I have from my mother's side Jewish background, from my father's side a very Catholic background. My mother had to defect in the second world war when the Russians invaded her town in Czechoslovakia. She was in a camp in Germany....Heidelberg. She slept in tents for years. That's part of me. That's my background. So, therefore, I'm everything a little bit. That's probably why I'm more open-minded than most people."

Unfortunately, these days Becker doesn't seem interested in continuing to embrace his connection to Judaism. When I tried to chat with him about his mother at the 2013 U.S. Open, he told me "I don't talk about that." When I suggested he allow me to explain why I was asking so he could make an informed decision as to whether he wanted to address the subject, he repeated "I don't talk about that."

Why Becker has decided it's not a topic of conversation any longer is something he's not chosen to reveal so we can only wonder what brought about the turnaround.

Two longtime journalist colleagues have periodically checked in with where I was at in the writing stage of the book. They both inquired as to whether I spoke with Becker and had these reactions to Becker's reaction regarding his mother. The first, who interviewed Becker frequently in his playing days, simply stated, "He's in denial now." The second remembered what his Jewish father always told him, "If you lived in Hitler's Germany and the knock came at the door at 2:00 a.m. to take you away, you can bet you were Jewish."

Pete Sampras

When asked to describe his family background, Pete Sampras says he's three-quarters Greek and one-quarter Jewish. In actuality, if we're judging Pete's heritage according to traditional beliefs he'd be considered half-and-half as his father, Sam, was born to a Jewish mother. While Pete was raised in the Greek Orthodox faith, he always remembers his Jewish lineage. One year during the Miami tournament, Sampras went to the famed Miami Seaquarium to do a question-and-answer period with local children. One child in the audience asked Pete what he is and Pete responded that he has a Greek and Jewish history. It doesn't appear Pete had much Jewish teachings — maybe Grandma made matzoh ball soup — but coming from Southern California he likely went to a number of Bar-and-Bat Mitzvahs as a child.

Rafael Nadal

Not that long ago, the Internet was alive with the suggestion that Rafael Nadal Parera might have a Sephardic Jewish heritage. The reasoning was that back in the time of the Spanish Inquisition, many Mallorcan Jews were forced to convert to Catholicism and take new family names. It is known the converted often chose the names Parera and Nadal as their new last names.

I asked my friend, ATP Tour Communications Senior Vice President Nicola Arzani, if he would approach Nadal and ask him whether the rumors were at all plausible. I specifically asked Nicola to intercede as although Nadal's English has dramatically improved, it is no secret he feels more comfortable speaking in his native Spanish. And I wanted to make sure that Rafa was presented with the question in Spanish so he understood what was being asked.

Nadal, it turns out, wasn't surprised by Arzani's query. In fact, the family was aware of the history of Sephardic Jews and had wondered themselves about the possibility they might have a Jewish past. Rafa told Nicola that his grandfather had done some research regarding both sides of the family — the Nadals on his father's side, the Pareras on his mother's side — but hadn't turned up any evidence that pointed to a Jewish ancestry. How his grandfather went about the research and how far back he was able to dig is not known, but it could be an interesting pursuit for a genealogy specialist.

Torben Ulrich

Torben Ulrich, the man with long flowing hair that many in tennis have referred to as the world's first tennis hippie, was a Danish tennis player. His parents — Einer and Ulla — were both tennis players. Ulla Meyer was from a Jewish family and when the Nazis came to Denmark, Einer arranged passage for Ulla and their two sons to Sweden, but they were caught en route by the Germans. Einer was able to negotiate a deal to get them out and the entire family eventually made passage to Sweden where they stayed until returning to Denmark after World War II. Torben, who became the oldest Davis Cup participant in history just one month shy of his 49th birthday in 1977, is the father of Metallica drummer Lars Ulrich.

Michael Russell

The American Michael Russell's mother is Jewish, but he was raised and identifies himself as a Methodist, which is his father's religion.

Jay Lapidus

Lapidus, who played at Princeton and on the tour in the 1980s, was born to a non-Jewish mother and Jewish father. He wasn't raised within the Jewish faith.

Luke and Murphy Jensen

When Luke and Murphy Jensen's mother, Patricia, went back to Lithuania to research her roots she discovered that some of her ancestors were Jewish. When I inquired of Murphy about his mother's discovery, he confirmed the information and seemed intrigued — and welcoming — to his newly discovered Jewish heritage.

Mardy Fish

Nope, Mardy isn't Jewish, not even with a last name of Fish. But he married Stacey Gardner, a Jewish attorney/ former briefcase model on NBC's TV show "Deal or No Deal" from Los Angeles. The couple was married at the Four Seasons Hotel in a traditional Jewish ceremony in September 2008. During one Passover after Fish's marriage, Justin Gimelstob attended a Gardner family Passover seder and posted a photo on social media of Fish, the youngest in the room, reading the Four Questions.

At the April 2011 Sony Open in Miami, Marvin Glassman, a reporter for a number of Jewish publications, asked Fish a question regarding his future children. Unfortunately, Glassman's timing to bring up the subject wasn't ideal as Fish had just lost to Novak Djokovic in the semifinals. But Marvin has never been shy in getting his Jewish-related questions out there.

Marvin Glassman: "I was looking for research on you, and I know that a couple years ago when you got married you were in this Jewish ceremony and you broke the wine glass. Were you thinking of converting to Judaism or raising your children as Jews?"

Mardy Fish: "I think isn't it whatever the wife is? I don't know. We're a ways away. She's probably going to win that argument anyway. Hopefully, they'll be both." Mardy and Stacey welcomed their first child, son Beckett Gardner Fish, to the family in February 2014.

JEWS AROUND THE GAME

There have been — and continue to be — many Jewish people who have had important and essential positions in the game. Here are a few of the Jewish players in the game who weren't actual players.

Joseph F. Cullman III

Joseph Cullman was the chairman and chief executive of Philip Morris and in that position was instrumental in the growth of the women's game. He provided the sponsorship and financial backing to create the women's own Virginia Slims Circuit, and also served as a president and chairman of the International Tennis Hall of Fame.

Gladys Medalie Heldman

A serious tennis player, and the mother of former tour player Julie Heldman, Gladys Heldman was the driving force behind the birth of the women's Virginia Slims Circuit, bringing her friend, Joseph Cullman III, in to sponsor the first women's professional tour. Heldman also founded *World Tennis* magazine in 1953, and served as the publisher, editor-in-chief and writer of the publication until selling the periodical in the 1970s.

Ian Froman

A South African dentist, Ian Froman went to Israel to play in the 1961 Maccabiah Games as an enthusiastic amateur tennis player of note. He fell in love with the country and not only eventually moved to the Holy Land, but became the driving force in the establishment of the Israel Tennis Center.

Anthony Lewisohn Godsick

Tony Godsick began his career as a sports agent at the International Management Group. He has been the agent and good friend to Roger Federer since the outset of the Swiss sensation's career and the two now are partners in their own sports agency, Team8, which counts Federer and Juan Martin del Potro among its clients. Godsick is married to former tour player Mary Joe Fernandez and the couple has two children.

Jerry Solomon

Jerry Solomon started his career working at ProServ and Ivan Lendl became one of his most high-profile clients. He left ProServ in 1994 and started StarGames, his own sports marketing and management company, which is based in Boston. He is an instrumental force in the development of World Tennis Day that has events taking place around the globe in early March. He is married to Olympic ice skating silver medalist Nancy Kerrigan and they have three children. He also has a son from a previous marriage.

David Markin

David Markin, the former owner and CEO of Checker Motors Corporation, the iconic taxi cab manufacturer, served as the chairman of the board and president of the United States Tennis Association in 1989-1990.

Alan Schwartz

Alan Schwartz, the founder and owner of Chicago's Midtown Tennis Club, the world's largest indoor tennis facility, served as the chairman of the board and president of the United States Tennis Association in 2003-2004.

Jon Vegosen

Jon Vegosen, a partner in the Chicago law firm of Funkhouser Vegosen Liebman and Dunn Ltd., served as the chairman of the board and president of the United States Tennis Association in 2011-2012.

Larry Scott

Scott, an All-American at Harvard, started his career in tennis as a player, reaching a career high singles ranking of No. 210 and winning one doubles title at Newport in 1987. He moved into the business side of the game at the ATP, advancing to President and Chief Operating Officer of ATP Properties, a division of the men's tour. Scott then became the Chairman & Chief Executive Officer of the women's WTA and was instrumental in bringing in key sponsorship from Sony Ericcson, Whirlpool, Gatorade, etc. Scott currently serves as the Commissioner of the Pac-12 Conference in college sports.

Marilyn and Ed Fernberger

The Fernbergers, who met while attending the University of Pennsylvania, spent 25 years of their 63-year marriage as an American force in tennis. They were co-chairmen of the U.S. Pro Indoor tournament held in Philadelphia each year and all the greats, including Rod Laver, John Newcombe, Arthur Ashe, Jimmy Connors, Bjorn Borg, and John McEnroe played the tournament. In 1988, the Fernbergers extended a wildcard into the tournament to a 16-year-old Pete Sampras having heard of his promise. Two years later, Sampras was back at Philadelphia to win his first career title. The Fernbergers served on the Board of Directors of the International Tennis Hall of Fame and funded a number of charities through tournament proceeds.

Ken Solomon

The Chairman and Chief Executive Officer of the Tennis Channel, Ken Solomon parlayed his long career as a show business executive into growing the independent cable network dedicated to tennis 24/7. Through Solomon's involvement, Tennis Channel now is a network player at the four majors and other premier events such as his hometown tournament at Indian Wells - Solomon graduated from Palm Springs High School. Prior to the Tennis Channel, Solomon was a President of Universal Studios Television, and also had executive positions with DreamWorks, Scripps and News

Corp. Known as a political animal, Solomon maintains a close relationship with President Barack Obama and serves as a member of the prestigious President's Committee on the Arts and the Humanities.

Ken Meyerson

Ken Meyerson, a native of Montreal, Canada, joined the tennis tour as a sports agent fairly soon after his college graduation from the American University in Paris with a BA in Business Administration. His first job was with ProServ in 1987 and from there worked at a number of other well-known companies, ending up as the president of Lagardere Unlimited's tennis division. Through the years, Meyerson represented many top draw clients, including Stefan Edberg, Jimmy Connors, Yannick Noah, Michael Stich, Andy Roddick, Justine Henin, Fernando Gonzalez, Mardy Fish and Shahar Pe'er. Meyerson tragically died in his sleep at his home in Miami, Fla., at age 48 in October 2011. Upon hearing the news of Meyerson's death, Roddick tweeted, "Ken. I love you and miss you. I will forever be grateful for you faith & loyalty. You will forever be my brother. As always 'Thanks Meyerson.'"

A FINAL WORD

Jews and Tennis Do Belong Together

There are those who will ask: Why is this book necessary? Why is it important? There are actually a number of answers to those questions.

Purely from a writer's perspective, the topic provided a vehicle for which the interesting personal stories of the players within these pages could be told. In truth, many of them have nothing in common beyond the fact they are all tennis players and all Jewish. But that's enough of a shared thread to bring them together in this book. And that, in and of itself, provided a writer with a worthy project to pursue. And yes, sometimes it is all about you.

That said, there are, without a doubt, more relevant reasons to write a book about the best Jewish tennis players in history.

Throughout history, the Jews have not been wholly revered for their athletic prowess. Stereotypically, those of the Jewish faith are noted for being bookish — scholarly and savvy at school and work. Who hasn't heard that every Jewish mother wants her son to be a doctor — the old joke even includes that mama won't be as pleased about her son the lawyer. There's also the well-known belief that Jews just don't do sports, and for good reason, in that those of the Jewish faith come complete with two left feet.

In the book *Emancipation through Muscles: Jews and Sports in Europe*, edited by Michael Brenner and Gideon Reuveni, in the introduction, Jews and Sports, Brenner asks: "JEWS AND SPORTS? We all know how much Jews contributed to the cultural heritage of humankind, from Freud in the realm of psychology and Einstein in the natural sciences all the way to Marx in politics, Kafka in literature, and Schonberg in modern music. But Jews and sports? Do they really go together?"

To a certain extent, at least in days of yesteryear, the Jewish communities themselves shied away from devoting much effort to dispelling the impression that Jews were klutzy and not meant to be star athletes. The element of concern at Jews playing sports had nothing to do with the competitive nature of athletics. The apprehension for some was based on sports being a portal to assimilation, which could result in the watering down of the Jewish way of being, even possibly threatening Jewish survival.

As recently as Wimbledon 2013, Nathan Abrams in a HAARETZ.com article "For Jews On Film The Tennis Lawn Is Always Greener" writes: "As the greatest tennis tournament in the world — Wimbledon — reaches its climax, it's an apt time to pause and consider the symbolism of the sport for Jews. The relationship between the court and the Chosen People is a complicated one, perhaps best illustrated on films, where the propriety and ritual of the game has served as a visual stand-in for the elusive world of the goy."

Indeed, in literature and in Hollywood, Jewish authors, screenwriters and directors have at times paid homage to a number of stereotypes related to those of the Jewish faith via the use of tennis, a sport considered to be favored by the genteel, upper crust of society.

The comedy classic "Airplane" called attention to the notion that Jews were a minority in the world of sports superstars in the scene where a flight attendant offers a "Famous Jewish Sports Legends" brochure to a passenger who requests something that would be light reading.

Woody Allen employs tennis as a way to show the desire of Jews to assimilate into a world of higher society in a number of films, including the 1979 film "Annie Hall," and he even used a distinctly tennis term to name his 2005 film "Match Point." In "Annie Hall," one way Allen's character Alvy Singer finds he doesn't belong with the dynamic and WASPY Annie (played by Diane Keaton) is by his ineptness at tennis.

In the movie "Goodbye Columbus," an adaptation from the Philip Roth satire novella of the same name, tennis also is a vehicle. It shows the difference between the nouveau riche Jewish family relocated to the suburbs and the more traditional middle-class Jews remaining in the city when Brenda (Ali McGraw), the Radcliffe College attending daughter of the upwardly mobile Patimkin family, tells working class Neil Klugman (Richard Benjamin) to meet her at the tennis court for their first date. Neil sits on a bench and watches Brenda and her fellow Ivy Leaguer friend playing until it becomes too dark to continue. In a nod to the desire to assimilate, Neil inquires why Brenda never approaches the net. She responds that she doesn't want to risk being hit by the ball and risk damaging her nose job, suggesting in the past she had a more ethnically-shaped facial feature.

In reality, however, we all know, stereotypes can be seriously flawed and based on assumed prejudices. And when it comes to Jews and their capability as athletes, that is definitely the case — there are great, good and not-so-great athletes that are and aren't Jewish.

Obviously, there's no doubt there are far more famous non-Jewish athletes than Jewish athletes, including in tennis. That can hardly be surprising as the world's Jewish population is estimated to only be 0.19 percent of the overall global population by the Anti-Defamation League.

The truth is that through the years there have been many Jews who've made a name for themselves by using their brawn — along with their brains — to become world-class athletes, including within the sport of tennis. And this book tells their story — and celebrates — the achievements of the many Jews from all corners of the Earth that found their footing on this planet by wielding a tennis racket.

NOTE FROM THE PUBLISHER

New Chapter Press wants to acknowledge David Goodman, the former executive director of the USTA Eastern Section, for helping to inspire this book. Goodman originally compiled a list of the great Jewish tennis players who won Grand Slam tournament titles. Goodman's work was published in 2010 as an article called "The A to Z Guide To Jewish Grand Slam Champions" on www.TennisGrandstand.com.

We encourage debate and contributions to this subject and welcome readers to share thoughts and comments on this book via social media on Twitter at @JewishTennis and on Facebook at www.facebook.com/JewishTennisBook.

We also encourage you to review our book on Amazon.com to help others learn about the benefits of this book. Your feedback helps improve the quality of our books. Thank you!

ALSO FROM NEW CHAPTER PRESS

A Backhanded Gift
By Marshall Jon Fisher

Love, tennis, sex, frustrated artistic ambition, and the dilemma of being a German Jew are all ingredients of this literary delight that is at turns serious and comedic. A novel written by the author of the book *A Terrible Splendor: Three Extraordinary Men, A World Poised For War and the Greatest Tennis Match Ever Played*, this romantic tale is set in the Jewish tennis community in 1980s Munich, Germany.

Titanic: The Tennis Story
By Lindsay Gibbs

A stirring and remarkable story, this novel tells the tale of the intertwined life of Dick Williams and Karl Behr who survived the sinking of the Titanic and went on to have Hall of Fame tennis careers. Two years before they faced each other in the quarterfinals of the U.S. Nationals – the modern-day U.S. Open - the two men boarded the infamous ship as strangers. Dick, 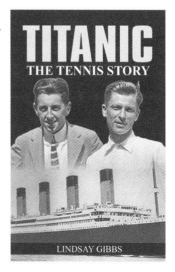 shy and gangly, was moving to America to pursue a tennis career and attend Harvard. Karl, a dashing tennis veteran, was chasing after Helen, the love of his life. The two men remarkably survived the sinking of the great vessel and met aboard the rescue ship Carpathia. But as they reached the shores of the United States, both men did all they could to distance themselves from the disaster. An emotional and touching work, this novel brings one of the most extraordinary sports stories to life in literary form. This real-life account – with an ending seemingly plucked out of a Hollywood screenplay - weaves the themes of love, tragedy, history, sport and perseverance.

The Greatest Tennis Matches of All Time
By Steve Flink

Author and tennis historian Steve Flink profiles and ranks the greatest tennis matches in the history of the sport. Roger Federer, Billie Jean King, Rafael Nadal, Bjorn Borg, John McEnroe, Martina Navratilova, Rod Laver, and Chris Evert are all featured in this book that breaks down, analyzes, and puts into historical context the most  memorable matches ever played. Practically providing readers with a courtside seat at tennis' most historic and significant duels, this resource is sure to be the start—and end—of many tennis debates.

The Education of a Tennis Player
By Rod Laver with Bud Collins

Depicting the monumental achievements of a world-class athlete, this firsthand account documents Rod Laver's historic 1969 Grand Slam sweep of all four major tennis titles. Co-authored with renowned tennis expert Bud Collins, this frank memoir details Laver's

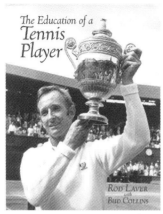

childhood, early career, and his most important matches. Each chapter also contains a companion tennis lesson, providing tips on how players of all levels can improve their own game and sharing strategies that garnered unparalleled success on the courts. Fully updated on the 40th anniversary of the author's most prominent triumph, this revised edition contains brand new content, including the story of Laver's courageous recovery from a near-fatal stroke in 1998.